AF271727

BOYhOOD

&

BEYOND

A MEMOIR

GLENN THEBERGE

A Memoir Boyhood & Beyond

©2023, Glenn Theberge

All rights reserved. This book or any portion thereof may not be reproduced or used in any manner whatsoever without the express written permission of the publisher except for the use of brief quotations in a book review.

ISBN: 978-1-66789-213-9

ISBN eBook: 978-1-66789-214-6

TABLE OF CONTENTS

1

GEMS AND SHARDS

2

PUBESCENCE

3

JUVENILITY

4

WINGING IT

5

MISHAPS AND ILLUMINATIONS

6

MOVING FORWARD

7

RUMINATIONS

8

LOOKING UP

ONE

GEMS AND SHARDS

PIECES OF A JOURNEY

"Dad, you should write this stuff down." These are the words I hear so often from my children. So I started. English was one of my least-liked classes in school. Reading was a strong contender, blah. I guessed I could put ink on paper if cats swim.

Burnt toast, black, crusty, charred aroma. My first writings were like that. Then several years ago, I saw an adult enrichment class offered by the College of Southern Idaho (C.S.I.)- Non-fiction Creative Writing. A published poet & English Professor & Drama Instructor co-taught the course. They specialize in teaching cats to swim.

I hope this memoir can put a smile on your face, reveal the changing world, and maybe conjure up memories to reflect on and share.

I dared to remove my clothes. Some attitudes and thoughts are offensive. Not proud. But real.

Can a cat be saved from drowning and groomed to be respectable?

What began as a few scrapbook childhood memories for my family evolved into personal pieces of a life journey. Gems and shards of actions, thoughts, and attitudes, none of which are hidden from the One above. The adventure, as I see it, has spiritual significance.

"Dad, I can't believe you said that." Or, "Did you really do that?" Or, "I never told you…." What will the response be? A slap on the face, a hug, tears, resentment…? Enjoy!

TWO

PUBESCENCE

NAILED

Sandy blond hair, thin short legs, and a smile on my face, mom sent me out on a mission.

"Glenn, I want you to go visit Mrs. Lawson. If she is not home, stop by Mrs. Perkins, I'm sure they would enjoy your company."

Mom gazed out the doorway as I scurried up the asphalt driveway toward the concrete sidewalk. The pitter-patter of my little Buster Brown shoes rounded the corner out of mom's sight.

I visited Mrs. Lawson several times with mom. She is an old, tubby widow with a cane and a warm, friendly smile. On the flip side, her neighbor, Mrs. Perkins, is a skinny, small, frail widow with a much different demeanor. I was less familiar with the grouch; memories of her yelling at Roger, her neighbor, my friend, and me whenever the football went in her yard.

Mrs. Lawson's home was about half a block from my house down the tree-lined busy Route 150. Mrs. Perkin's abode was just the next house past.

I stopped on the sidewalk for a moment to get my bearings. The aroma of Widow Lawson's oven-baked cookies was overcome by curiosity. Something caught my eye. Under the shadow of the trees, just past the Lawson house. A clump lying on the frost-heaved concrete. *I thought, no hurry, I will see what this is.* Step by step, slowly, I approached the cluster until I straddled it. Yep, sure enough, just as I thought. A sharp nail right in the middle of the small water-stained wood scrap. I stood there for a moment, pondering. *I wonder if I stood on this spike with these strong Buster Brown shoes, would the nail hold me up, or would it pierce my shoe. Maybe I could balance on it like an acrobat.*

I carefully raised my right foot while keeping my balance with my left foot firmly planted. I aimed my right foot directly over the top of the nail, carefully placing the center of my right sole to touch the tip of the rusty nail. I was ready to test my theory; the strength of my sole and the nail would hold me. Slowly shifting my weight, then with haste, I pressed down with pressure until I could feel the nail gripping my right shoe's bottom. Then I raised my left foot and stood on the nail.

"Oh, fudgesicles, poopy, poopy." My eyes welled up, and tears streamed down my face.

I sat down and tried to pull the intruder out of my foot. No luck. The penetration was too deep, and my little arms were not strong enough. I stood on my left leg, got part of the board under my left foot, and then tried to pull my right foot up off the nail. No luck.

Sobbing the words, "poopy, poopy, poopy," I headed back home. Clapity clap, clapity clap. Up the porch steps.

Mom came to the rescue. Not a frown or raised eyebrow, but wide eyes and compassion filled her face.

"Glenn, what on earth did you do? What's happened to you? Come here. Let me help you."

She sat my skinny butt down on the chair.

"It hurts, mom, it hurts. It's stuck."

She tugged and twisted on that board until it came free. She removed Buster Brown and my sock to find only a red spot, no blood. A change of footwear, and off I go. I love my liberty and am on my way again to another adventure.

I thank God for giving me such a caring and compassionate mom.

DUPED

At seventy-one, remembering a story from when I was six years old is like looking at a photo through a muddy puddle, but I need to tell it.

I was messing around on the front lawn and eating candy; M&M's, Junior Mints, Malted Milk balls, gumballs, I'm not sure what. It was a bright sunny day. A tall man (everybody is tall when you're six) walked by the house on the town sidewalk. He was nicely dressed and had a friendly face. He stopped and turned toward me, about ten feet away. He saw me munching on my treats. I looked up at him and paused.

"Hey, boy," he said. "Do you like candy?"

I took a small step forward and said, "Yeah, I like candy."

He replied, "Come here. I got some for you."

He reached into the pocket of his long button-up tweed coat and pulled out three gumball size white balls. He extended an open hand.

"Here," he said, "take these. They are very yummy."

I strolled to the nice man, who handed me the round morsels.

With a big smile, I clenched them in my hand and said, "Thank you, I love gumballs."

He said, "You're welcome. Enjoy them."

He zipped away toward town out of sight. I turned, walked back into my yard, and leaned against the tall fat pine tree. I pinched one of the free candies between my short, nimble fingers and thumb and stuffed it into my mouth. An antiseptic odor caught my attention as the smooth white ball quickly passed under my nose. But too late, the dreadful poison was already smashed between my teeth, and the granules coated my tongue. I ran to the side of the house and hid in the corner.

"Oh yuck!" I spit it out. I spit- over and over until the horrible taste was mostly gone. But the mothball taste lingered. After my tears dried up, I came out of the corner and tried to eat some more candy and mess around in the yard again, but it wasn't the same. My day was ruined.

Mothballs, who even uses them anymore? I can still smell them with just the thought. Strangers… hmm. Kids should listen to their mothers.

THE BOYS IN THE WOOD

The naked boy stood by the edge of the country road, mortified, not daring to move. Bill's mother's eyes were fixed on him, ready to give more consequences for disobedience. An occasional motorist that passed by nearly swerved off the narrow pavement. Bill was so embarrassed, standing there, naked for all to see.

He must have thought, why isn't Glenn here to share this shame with me? I wonder what pain he is suffering. Maybe none, I bet, just a finger wagging in the face or some kind of lecture.

So why was Bill standing at the edge of the road in his birthday suit?

The chicken coop stood 30 yards behind the house, nestled against the forested acres of an abandoned logging project. Bill's parents purchased the wooded property a few years ago and built their three-bedroom cape-style home there. The several miles from town gave them the privacy they yearned for. Their closest neighbor was a 1/4 mile away. Their dogs could run wherever, and the cats could chase chipmunks. The chickens ran free until the neighbor's dogs and the fox began their feasting.

The backwoods, the meandering brook, and the old logging roads were a haven for adolescents. The peacefulness and quiet among the trees and brush leave room for curiosity to bloom. Gay was not part of the equation.

Who knows why boys do what boys do. Nakedness in the wild. It's as natural as climbing a tree in a lightning storm.

Bill's mom, Pauline, was at ease with him being gone unattended for hours on end, knowing that the 4th. grader would always come home when he got hungry. She would occasionally venture from her kitchen table. She left her chocolate cake, coffee, and Whitman chocolates to check on Bill if she determined too much time had passed. This was one of those days. A dreadful day it was.

Pauline waddled across the backyard and into the woodland looking for Bill and me.

"Bill," I whispered, "I hear someone coming!"

Bill replied," Shhhhhhhh, don't move."

"Oh no, too late," I said.

Just past the chicken coop, concealed in a group of pine, the rustling branches had caught her ear. The gremlin approached. Her eyes grew huge, her jaw dropped, her face became scarlet, and the veins in her neck popped like corrugated metal. "What are you boys doing?" Bill and I learned some new words as we put on our clothes. The march to the house was swift.

Pauline dialed my mother. "Elaine! Get your perverted son. Come get him right now, right now!"

Mom responded, "Why? What's wrong?"

"Just get over here, get your ass over here, now. You'll see when you get here. Just get over here."

By the time mom arrived, Bill was standing stark naked at the edge of the road.

Bill and I remain friends. But as life happens, our lives drift apart; College, Vietnam, marriage, re-locating…. One of Bill's passions came to fruition. Bill and his wife bought a nudist colony. This town boy decided to wear the costume of commonality.

TAKEN BY SURPRISE

I stood there, almost naked. Wearing only my tight white Fruit of the Loom skivvies. Seven soldiers were staring at me. Four from inside and three from outside - gawking through the doorway. It happened so fast I didn't have time to be embarrassed.

Earlier that day, eight of us were banded together, looking for something to do. We are called the baby boomer generation; consequently, the small town of Amesbury is populated with hundreds of kids my age. That was over sixty years ago. We attended different schools. Some went to one of the two Catholic schools; Sacred Heart or Saint Joseph. The others to public schools; the Ordway, the Bartlet, and the Horace Man School. I attended Whittier elementary.

Most youngsters didn't know that Catholics and Protestants were not supposed to be comrades. There were prejudice and religious bias among many adults. But some marriages were mixed; protestant and catholic. As kids, we just hung out together and did our thing unless our parents objected.

This was a perfect day to play army. After a bit of heated debate, we decided to draw straws to see who would be captains. Bill & Wayne, the brothers from across the street, pulled the longest straws and were named. They took turns and picked their squads. We grabbed our

machine guns, rifles, knives, and hand grenades, and headed out to claim our territories.

Some time passed, and our team got anxious as we had not seen the enemy's helmet nor boot. So we headed out to hunt down Billie's gang. We began combing the neighborhood, careful not to disturb the grouchy old neighbor on the corner, Mrs. Merrill. She didn't like ten-year-olds running through her yard and flowers and jumping over her white picket fence. We found that out the hard way—an event not to be repeated. Instead, we headed around the backside of Maude's house, the old widowed lady. She was much more tolerant than Mrs. Merrill, though she did stand on the porch and scream at us occasionally.

The neat thing about Maude's place is that she owns a big old chestnut tree in her backyard. The thorny, prickly outer shells-our source of hand grenades. Caution, wear gloves and handle with care. Thorns may cause severe injury.

Our troops were headed toward the enemy's backyard, a likely hide-out spot. It's a large, wide open grass area not very well kept with tall grass. A couple of elms there give good shade and are fit for climbing. There are a few small dirt mounds in the middle of the yard for cover. There is also a little shack (also known as the smokehouse, centered in the yard; more about smoking later). As we were scouting the yard, Wayne spotted them. They were hunkered down in the stinky eight-foot by eight-foot old plywood strong-hold. He saw movement through the one small wood window.

Wayne pointed and said quietly. "There they are. We've got them now. Let's surround them."

"Have they seen us?" I whispered.

"Not yet. Scatter, take cover, and go on my signal," Wayne muttered.

Wayne took cover behind the giant tree. The other guys hid low in the tall grass and weeds. I rushed toward the dirt mound close to the shack. The enemy spotted me and opened fire. I made it to the sandy mound and took cover. I laid still for several minutes.

"We got 'em now," Wayne said. "Just hold on for a little bit. I'll give a signal; we'll charge all at once."

I began screaming, "Ooh, ow, dang, ouch, my ankle, ah, my leg, my arm, my neck. What the heck! Ooh, ow man, they're all over me." I jumped up, ran, and burst through the shack door. I ripped off my tee shirt, shoes, and socks. Then my pants.

"Ah, ow, ah!" I tearfully declared. All the time, slapping and brushing off the six-legged red things.

"Fire ants." I screamed, "They're fire ants."

The whole army was standing there with their mouths open, wide-eyed, dazed, watching what the heck was going on. The biting stopped.

The troops finally figured out what was happening. I shook out my clothes and put them back on.

We discovered the "fire ants" owned that little sandy mound. The tiny red things had covered my whole body, going up my pants, in my socks, and under my shirt from head to toe, and were eating me, devouring me alive, one bite at a time, hundreds of them.

The days of playing guns and war are far behind me. I enjoyed my childhood, days of adventure and fun. The world is such a different place now for kids and adults. But the battles of unforeseen challenges and surprises linger on.

TROUBLE

"Mom, no, I didn't mean it. She was in the way. It's not my fault. It's not fair."

By age ten, I had perfected my ability to tease and annoy my sister, like poking a wasp nest. I was pleased to hear her scream or holler, "Mom!" My only sister Donna is four years younger, which gives me an extreme advantage.

We lived in a clapboard and wood-shingled two-story home one mile from town on Market Street, also known as Highway 150. Mom still lives there. My bedroom is upstairs at the end of the hall across from Mom and Dad's room. Little sister's is at the head of the stairs, and my brother, Ted's room, is in the middle. My brother Ted, three years younger than me, had cerebral palsy, so he was off-limits to my shenanigans. It would have been nice to have a mate. What wolf pup preys alone?

My bedroom floor is covered with tan linoleum printed with cars, buses, bridges, boats, planes, and trains. Its thinly striped border is blue and red. This scheming room's north and east windows have bone-white roll-up vinyl shades, and white sheer Dacron curtains pulled back and tied in the middle. Still the same as in 1959. The east window is my favorite. It has a street view and a tall pine tree with branches close to the front porch roof below the window. The tree is now gone. I climbed down that tree once to sneak out of the house. My chamber walls are now pink. I don't know when that happened. The metal desk has vanished, and the other furniture has been replaced with antique bureaus and storage boxes. I particularly remember the metal bed that was there. The head and footboard's top rails were large arched-shaped pipes with round vertical metal bars closely and evenly spaced. Narrowly spaced.

The memory is imprisoned in my mind. That dreadful day Mom sent me to my room. Teasing is why. Punished by Mom. What loving Mom doesn't discipline their son? My Mom showed her love to me quite often. On this day, I spent my time gazing out the bedroom windows lying on that cold steel-framed bed.

After lying on the bed for eternity, I became bored and began thinking of ways to pass the time until my sentence was completed. *I wonder whether my head will would fit between the bars.* I scooted my body toward the foot of the bed. Then pushed my head between the vertical metal rods. Squeezing my ears through up to my neck where there was a little more room. Less pressure and more mobility. I turned on my back and got comfortable. *Ah, this is nice.* I became tired of this position after fifteen minutes. I decided to do something else while waiting to complete my punishment. I turned onto my stomach and tried to remove my head from between the bars. Stuck. I tried lying on my back, from the fetal position, on my stomach again, moaning, pushing, pulling… still stuck. *That's it. I better get help.*

"Mom, Mom, help."

Mom's loud response from downstairs came after several requests, "It's not time to get up yet."

My pleas continued like consuming cotton candy. Finally, I heard stomping coming up the stairs, then muttering in the hall outside my bedroom door.

"Mom, Mom, help," as the door flew open.

She gasped, "Oh my God, what have you done?" After a few minutes of mother magic, I was released from captivity, ending my sentence. Free at last. Free to continue years of pleasantry. I love my little armored sister.

A MOMENT FROM THE PAST

The photograph, in my mind, has ragged edges and is a bit faded. But the impression remains. I flip through the album in my mind to put together a collage.

I sit on the front porch steps and watch a car pull up to the gas pumps at Frazier's' garage- a brother-owned service station and Pontiac dealership. Two Mobile Pegasus leaded-fuel pumps are mounted on an oval red concrete island in front of the establishment.

"Ding, ding," sounds as the car runs over the long black rubber hose that stretches across the pavement and through the bottom of the island to the other side of the pumps.

Kris Kellogg, a large rugged, slightly plump man dressed in neatly pressed khaki trousers and a button-up shirt soiled on the sleeves, approached the vehicle as the driver cranked down the window.

"Filler up, ma'am?"

"No, not today, Kris. Stop at $3."

"O.K.," he said with a big smile and a tip of his billed hat. "Oh, will that be regular or high test?"

"Make it regular."

Kris opened the gas flap door, removed the cover, and began putting in the three bucks.

"Mam, it only took $2.35."

She handed him $3.00.

"I'll get your change when I finish, ma'am."

"Fine, Kris, no hurry."

Kris lifted the hood, pulled out the dipstick, and checked the oil. He then removed the radiator cap.

"Waters a little low, ma'am."

Kris strolled over to the island, grabbed the galvanized long-spouted water can, and topped off the radiator. He closed the hood and wiped his greasy fingerprints off the Indian chief hood ornament. The stout, stogy puffing man raised the two windshield wiper blades, did a quick inspection, sprayed the windshield with light blue window cleaner, then wiped the windshield with the thick white paper towels from the dispenser attached to the island's flying horse signpost and lowered the wipers. He walked around to the other side of the car, where the air hose hung on the white cinder block building near the overhead service door. He turned the air machine handle to read thirty, then checked all four tires.

"I'll be right back with your change. The $2.35 filled her up, so I'll get you your S&H redemption green stamps."

Kris is a friendly guy. Except when I ride my twenty-four-inch green Columbia coaster braked bicycle over the ding, ding hose. When

he hears the ding, ding, then the ding, ding again, he drops what he is doing and trots outside to wait on the customer. I didn't mean to poke the hornet's nest.

One more piece of the collage; it's a warm day. I walk across our narrow driveway. The blacktop separates my porch steps from the service station. I meander to the Coke machine outside the building between the man door and the Pontiac showroom. Lester and Bob Frazier proudly display their antique, shiny two-tone red and maroon parade car behind the large picture windows.

I pose in front of the crimson and icy white round-shoulder machine and put my dime in the slot located above the dull grey twist knob. Clink, I hear the dime drop. My left-hand pulls the door open. I remove the small, green, shapely glass bottle decorated with the red and white banner. Grasping the sacred vessel of cold refreshment, I stick it in the door-mounted cap remover and pry off the lid. Fishhh, fizz. Some drool escapes from the corner of my lips.

Ahhhhh!

A tattered, small, yellow, wood-sided partitioned crate sits on the ground leaning on the building at an angle. I put the empty bottle in the box with the others.

TWENTY-FIVE CENTS

I peered into the small brown paper sack as I sat on my front steps. Mrs. Zeltzer, the plump straight-lipped Jewish store owner, had carefully put items into the bag so goodies wouldn't get smashed. I glanced across the street and saw the McFadden brothers hurling dog shit at each other from the end of sticks.

I'm smiling on the inside, thought the better of it. I remember what happened last weekend...

I had finished my Saturday chores; I swept the second floor and basement stairs, even in the corners. Then I took out the trash and emptied the garbage into the in-ground swill bucket. I detest stepping on the green metal peddle to open that thing, the maggots crawling, the putrid smell of rotting vegetables, the flurry of flies escaping... The pigman comes every Saturday afternoon. I can smell the truck a block away.

I scrambled down the front porch steps and headed across the street to join Wayne and Billy for catch football in their large backyard.

"Hey Billy, toss the ball to me," I'll run out for a long pass, "If you can throw it that far."

"Bet you can't catch it," Billy hollered.

"Try me," I yelled back.

Wayne piped up, "Hey guys, come here."

Billy and I headed over to meet Wayne.

When we approached Wayne, he whispered, "I've got something to show you. Come on. Let's go to the shack. You'll love this."

Billy pushed open the shabby solid wood door. The rotting eight-foot by eight-foot plywood floor bowed under our feet. Wayne gently closed the door and peered out the paint-peeled, glassless small wood window that faced the neighbor's house. Billy and I stared at Wayne, waiting. Wayne pulled a cigarette out of his pocket and fidgeted for the lighter.

"Hey, Billy, light the cig while I drag on it, you know, the way the old lady always does it."

Billy flicked the lighter and held it at the end of the cigarette until it glowed red. Wayne took a couple of drags, started coughing, and then took a few more puffs.

"Who wants to go next?" Wayne gasped.

"Give it to me," Billy demanded. Billy, the older brother, took a couple drags, inhaled, and blew smoke out his nose.

"That's how you do it," he exclaimed. "Glenn, it's your turn."

"Sure, I'll give it a try." I took a few drags and handed it to Wayne.

Wayne took a drag and gave it to Billy.

"You finish this," Wayne said to Billy. "I just saw the old lady take off for work, and I know where she stashes her cartons."

Wayne came back with a whole pack of Salem Menthols. He opened the pack and handed out the white filtered cigarettes. We all lit up and puffed away, practicing inhaling and blowing it out of our noses. Soon the shack filled with an ominous menthol cloud. My eyes watered, my head started swirling, and my throat became scratchy and sore.

"Wow," I exclaimed, "how much do you think these things cost?"

"A quarter a pack." Billy, the older one, responded. "But you have to be 21 to buy them."

Wayne butted in. "Can't get them at Seltzer's store. There's a place across town where we could ride our bikes, and no one would know we got them."

I woefully responded. "Ah. Not me. It would take a week's allowance to buy butts. I'm going home."

...so I watched the brothers from across the street, hurling and dodging the dog shit. I fished my change from the brown paper sack and put it in my corduroy jeans pocket. Then popped the bottle cap, ripped open the cellophane Twinkie wrapper, chomped down half of the first

finger of the sweet, yellow, rich cream-filled sponge cake, and washed it down with the tonic. *Mm, twenty-five cents, better spent and legal.*

ELEMENTARY SCHOOL

The well-dressed, stocky, red-faced man, his cheeks ready to burst, grabbed my red and white neatly pressed Roy Roger's shirt by the shoulders, gave a grunt, picked me up, and hung me by my collar on a coatroom hook. He is the meanest Principal ever. I don't remember what I did wrong to deserve such unjust punishment.

Whittier Elementary school, named after the famous poet John Greenleaf Whittier, is one of the four 1st to 4th Grade schools in the historic, small town of Amesbury, Massachusetts. It's almost a one-mile walk to school; no matter rain, wind, snow, or sun.

Every school day started the same. Mom would pack my lunch in a brown paper sack (there was no cafeteria). Sometimes I would get my favorite sandwich, a sweet and gooey fluffernutter-Skippy Chunky Peanut Butter smeared on Wonder Bread with Marshmallow Fluff. She would also comb my hair-hurricane proof; she did this using Wave Set. She would gently hold the end of the black-toothed comb between her thumb and finger and dip it into the jar. Most of the slimy green gel dripped off before she ran the comb through my hair to create a perfect part and a Hollywood wave. My hair dried rock hard-immovable.

When I got to school, I climbed up the numerous granite steps, entered the two-story pale yellow wooden building, turned to the left, and hung up my coat in the common coat room. I went to class and sat down in my assigned seat. After attendance, we stand up to put our hands over our hearts. The teacher led us in the Pledge of Allegiance of the 48-star flag, said the Lord's Prayer, and repeated Psalm 23. Mid-morning on Thursdays, banking day, the teacher passed out savings envelopes from the First National Bank. I deposited my 10 cents. Mid-morning each day was snack time in our classroom. I filled out the menu sheet for the next day and chose white or chocolate milk and a cookie. After the snack, it's out to the tree-shaded chain-linked fenced playground for recess. Boys on one side of the building and girls on the other side.

The twins, Kathy & Caroline Freeve, the prettiest girls in the class, always dressed alike. I couldn't tell them apart unless I stared them in the eyes. The one with the non-moving glass eye was Kathy. I liked the other one better, the girl, not the eye. Especially on Valentine's Day, I made sure Caroline got my anonymous Valentine's card. When Caroline sat in front of me, I loved tying her pigtails together.

Stanly Sweeny, the really odd kid in class, entertained me. One particular day I remember. He snatched a house fly right out of midair. He placed the creature on his desk, then pulled off its wings.

First, only one wing, so it buzzed around in circles on his desktop. Then he pulled off the other wing. The fly just stood there. After Stanley removed all its legs, he slowly pushed down on the fly with his thumb until its guts squeezed out.

When I was in 4th grade Mr. Mason, the strict, mean Principal, called my mother and requested a meeting with her at the school.

"Mrs. Theberge," He rattled off, "Your son can not stay awake in class. He is drained. He needs more sleep. Put him to bed earlier, so he can get more rest."

My Mother complied with his instruction. Bedtime became 6 pm. I watched the neighborhood kids play from my upstairs bedroom window until they all went home.

Mom has lived in that same house since 1952. A few years ago, I flew from Idaho to visit mom. During the visit, I took a walk to the old school. I stood as an empty vessel, staring.

The hook hanging by Mr. Mason and the pigtail tying is all muddy memory. Hmm, I do remember that the fly and the glass eye are right.

THREE

JUVENILITY

MORE THAN FIRE

Flickering, dancing pillars and tongues of red, orange, blue, and, sometimes, green or even white, reaching temperatures of incendiary proportions. When encompassed by a circle of stone or under rings of steel beneath a pan pose no threat. Often used to heat and roast those round white tasty morsels or boil varieties of edibles. But when they capture the imagination and fascination of elementary-age boys, it can be a whole different story. Especially when the experimentation of other uses takes place. Seeking to implement and enjoy some of those other creative fancies during my childhood, I share the following brainstorm we "cooked" up with you.

Not too far to the west and part way up Po Hill lived one of my school-mate buddies, Wayne Barbaro. We would walk to Prospect Elementary school together quite often. Sometimes we would hang out together after school or on the weekends. One Saturday morning, I showed up at Wayne's house, unsure what we would do that day or if he would be home. As was the custom those days, showing up unannounced would sometimes get your buddy out of doing chores for a while. Although, you were often disappointed because the parents were strict and sent you away till all the tasks were done.

Side note; Wayne's parents were the nicest people you would ever know, especially on the days when arriving. I could smell the aroma of Mrs. B's fresh-baked chocolate chip cookies hot out of the oven or whoopee pies (sweet white frosting cream sandwiched between two warm devils-food cakes). And I was invited to munch some down with a big glass of cold moo juice.

After the short hike partly up the hill and slightly out of breath, I took a deep breath and knocked. Sure enough, Shazam, Wayne answered the door; halleluiah, he was free. We decided we would play some one-on-one with the old pigskin. There was a nice, slightly sloped grassy spot just the right size in his yard. There were large bushes at each end. One side was bordered by the asphalt driveway and the other by a small hill. I wasn't dressed for the rough and tumble game of tackle. I had on one of my favorite sweaters, the long-sleeved blue one with the burlap textured vest design on the front. I loved that sweater. It was chilly this morning, so I elected to keep it on and be careful not to ruin it. Typical of elementary school kid thinking. I had two sets of clothes. One for school and one for play and unpleasant tasks. When I came home from school, I changed my clothes. I was in big trouble when I forgot to do that. I say when and not if. Because the excitement of getting home after school sometimes overruled my ability to think right.

Anyways, back to the game. We were having a great time kicking off to each other, running around, getting tackled, and tackling each other. Fake passing with a run play and all that.

Ka pomp, "Here it comes." Wayne yelled.

I hollered back. "Got it." Jetting down the field, about halfway with the end zone in sight, then, womp! I was sprawled out, pinned under the all-American defensive back, and lying face down on the turf. I started to feel something warm on my belly. The warmth intensified, also the smell of something burning. Smoke came out from under me.

"Oh man," I jumped up and realized my favorite sweater was burning. I quickly patted myself down and removed my button-up to ensure the cooking had stopped. There was a big old hole through the pocket, and the inside of the sweater was scorched.

You're probably wondering how a fourth-graders sweater would catch fire. I'll have to go back a few days to explain that.

I have no inkling where this idea came from. When Bob and I were at my house messing around, somehow, one of us, I can't remember which one came up with the idea of making a couple of match guns. Where did we get the plans? That's a mystery. I'm sure it wasn't out of the Boy Scout magazine or Good Housekeeping!

Bob and I took some spring-type pinching clothespins, disassembled them, and refashioned them into a gun. Then we took wooden matches and broke the heads off. Placed the match heads into the weapon, then shot. It was awesome. The match heads ignite, then fly about 10 yards. It's even better at night (I'm not sure if mom knows about the match guns. I'll have to ask her)

So back to the torched sweater. One of the days Bob and I were shooting our nifty inferno blasters, I was wearing that same sweater. As the custom in those days, we didn't put our clothes in the laundry until we wore them two times or more, as long as they weren't "dirty". I filled my sweater pocket with a lot of ammo, about half a box of wooden match heads. I didn't use them all and forgot I left the ammo in my pocket. So when my body hit the ground from the rugged special team's defense, the match heads ignited, resulting in one of the hottest football games on record.

Bob and I spent a lot of time together and invented many fun things. This is just one of the many exciting things we find to do to entertain ourselves. If I probe my memory, more of those times will come to mind.... Oh, yea, like when we scared the bejabbers from my sister. In the middle of the night, she heard voices coming from under her bed, and oh yea, then there was the time I woke my dad up from a sound sleep with blinding auto headlights in his bedroom! Oh yes, then there was the time........... Well, those stories are for another day.

Young boys are strange and marvelous creatures, aren't we? God has put this wildness, sense of adventure, and curiosity deep within our hearts. I guess sometimes we do some wild and stupid and crazy things. Not that they are all bad or good. It's the way He made us. We are fearfully and wonderfully made. To do good, wild, and crazy things.

So I think, where is this wild and crazy part of me? Has it gone somewhere? Is it lying in wait to be woken up? The lion sleeps only to roar again. Beware of boys and men!

TORMENTED AGAIN

Mom's stern rebuke sobered me but didn't discourage my passionate desire for future mischievous shenanigans.

Bob and I took the battery out of my old $15 "51" Ford field bomber. We set the battery next to the old car radio upstairs in my bedroom and began to tinker. Two adolescent boys and a dull afternoon evolved into the usual fiendish fantastic adventure.

"Hey Bob," I said, "I've got a cool idea. Let's scare my sister."

"I'm all in, Glenn. You know I love practical jokes, particularly to your little sister."

We put our heads together and made a plan.

"Hey Bob, My mom and sister will be home shortly, so we better get to it. This will be good."

Bob smiled with that, Bob, only impish grin, "I'll get the wire from the basement while you fetch the drill from your dad's shop."

I climbed up into the attic above the bedrooms while tall Bob drilled the hole in my closet ceiling.

"O.K. Bob, fish the wire up to me, and I'll run it over to Donna's room."

I climbed out of the attic and headed to my sister's room. We hooked the wires up to the radio speaker, hid it under the trash in the bedside waste paper basket, and connected the other end of the hidden wire to the old radio in my bedroom. Then connected the radio to the 12-volt car battery that I borrowed from my $15 Ford field bomber. We harmoniously broke out in unrestrained laughter.

The downstairs kitchen door closed with a bang. We muffled our merriment so there would not even hint of our plot to scare the bajibbies out of my sister.

Mom filled the kitchen with the aroma of fried pepper steaks, green peppers, onions, and potatoes, my favorite supper meal. Supper for all of us, including my extraordinary friend and overnight guest. Afterward, Donna and I did the dishes and cleaned up. Bedtime came just a few hours later. Bob and I lay there with haunting eyes in anxious anticipation until we knew she was asleep. Finally, all was still in the Theberge household.

I turned on the radio and waited.

Donna screamed, "Ahhhhhh, mom, someone is in my room!"

We heard mom scurrying up the stairs and quickly turned off the radio.

"What is it, Donna? What is it? What is it? What's wrong?"

"There is a man in my room. I heard him, a man under my bed or in the closet, in the radiator. I don't know, somewhere, I heard him!"

"I don't see anyone, Donna. I don't hear anything."

Donna's closet door squeaked open and closed several times. We could hear a little scuffling. Then silence. I turned the radio on again, and voices and music softly drifted down the hall.

"Shhhhhhhh," I whispered to Bob. "We are going to get caught."

"You Shhhhhh, Glenn," Bob growled.

Knock, knock on my door, then it opened wide. Mom burst into my bedroom.

"I hear you boys snickering under those covers. How dare you scare your sister like that. You're making those voices in her room, aren't you?! The man's voice, music, how are you doing that? Glenn, Bob? What's going on?!"

ALIEN MENACE

A woman, whose identity was not disclosed, came to the police station Sunday night and told officers, "There is something in the road, in the middle of Clinton Street...."

In Amesbury, Massachusetts, a small New England town located on the left bank of the Merrimac River near the mouth of the Atlantic Ocean, the 1649 Macy-Colby House exists today. Also, in the middle of town stands a memorial statue of Josiah Bartlett, a signer of our Declaration of Independence.

John Greenleaf Whittier's home, the author of "The Exiles,"-in which Thomas Macy is the subject, depicting the plight of the Quakers in the religious intolerant Puritan society, is located here.

Despite the rich history of this quaint New England town, there was not much excitement from a teenager's perspective in the 1960s. Unless you leave that up to Bob and me.

The September 1965 "Exeter Incident" inspired us to rise up out of our boredom. Bob and I have been friends for many years. We hung out on weekends.

This was Bob's senior year at Haverhill Trade school and my junior year at Amesbury High School. The trees were beginning to turn color, the morning air crisp, and the daylight hours getting shorter. We began scheming.

"Hey Bob, "We need to do something about this boredom."

Bob replied, "Yeah, something stunning."

I responded, "Yeah, something incredible. Got any ideas? How about something the whole town would know about. Something that would really raise eyebrows but not get us arrested."

We sat quietly, pondering.

Bob grinned, "Got it, a newspaper headline and a real eye-opener.

"I piped up, "What?"

Bob stood, looked me in the eye, and shouted, "Hey, how about this? Let's make a UFO."

I looked up at Bob and said, "A what?"

"A UFO, Glenn."

I stared at Bob as if he were a one-eyed, one-horned, flying purple people eater and said, "What do you mean, like a flying saucer?"

Bob replied with his Cheshire grin, "Yeah, not one that flies, but a fake one."

I rose to my feet, "That would be awesome. What a great idea. There's a lot of chatter about UFO sightings just five miles from here in Kensington. Yeah, what if one landed here in Amesbury? That would make headlines."

Bob's eyes lit up, his smile filled his face, and he said, "Let's build it and put it in the middle of the road someplace."

My knees began to tremble, "Yeah, Bob, let's do it."

Later that day, we ran to the "stone crusher" - an abandoned stone quarry in the woods at the north outer edge of town. The pine and the leafy forest is thick with gnarly underbrush divided by a creek from Powwow Hill, the 300-foot tall local six-rope-tow Skihill. The old quarry is a horse-shoe-shaped jagged rock wall with stony grass and a weedy clearing at the base. There is also a not-so-big shallow abandoned quarry, fifty bunny hops away. The "stone crusher" is a favorite hang-out and rock-climbing spot. We joined minds and forged a plan like undercover government agents.

Clinton Street was the perfect site for the Aliens to land. It's a frequently traveled stretch of unlighted narrow blacktop on the north end of town a couple miles south of the New Hampshire border. The chosen spot was a quarter-mile pavement between two large fields of tall grass. On the east part of the road is a hill, which creates a blind spot. On the west of the road is Highway 150, which leads north to Kensington.

Saturday morning, we walked to the "stone crusher." While strolling through the woods, we found a grove of young tall skinny pines.

"Bob, stop. Hey, we could use these saplings to make the legs."

"Say what?" Bob responded.

"Yeah, Bob, we can chop down these suckers and use them to make a huge cone. Tomorrow let's get our hatchets and do it. Let's get it going."

We found a clearing in the little crusher area, just the right place to build the UFO. We cut down the three straightest firs for the legs and delimbed them. The naked poles cried out from

the earth, "Stand me up. Stand me up." We stood up three 15-footers, lashed them together at the top with clothesline rope, and formed a tripod. Then Bob and I attached pine branches to broaden the cone.

Bob said, "There you go, that's how it's done."

I echoed, "Wow, that's awesome. Look at it from back here."

Bob proclaimed, "Keep going. We got to make this thing look bad."

I tiredly replied, "Maybe tomorrow."

Bob conceded, "Yeah, O.K. Let's cut out and catch some zees."

The next day we went to the construction site and plugged in our alien imaginations to complete the UFO. We also needed some coin to buy rad stuff.

I peered at Bob while sitting on the stump, "Hey, Bob, you got some allowance saved up?"

Bob tilted his head slightly and straightened his brows,

"What are you thinking?"

I stood erect, grinning, "I'm thinking tin foil, burlap, flashing lights."

Bob rose to his feet, "O.K., yeah, got it. Time to go shopping."

We went to Zeltser's (a Jewish mom-and-pop neighborhood grocery store next door to my home) and bought some of the dressing. Then to J.J. Newberry (a five-and-dime store chain) to buy the rest of the trimmings. The following weekend we went back to the sight.

Bob, "Looks like the one we see on TV. Can you believe it?"

Bob raised both hands and placed them on his head; all his teeth showed as he grinned from ear to ear, and his eyes widened, "I know it is outa sight, man. Turn that twirly light on; let's see how it looks."

"Hey Bob, that's awesome; I bet it shines even better a night. So now what?" Bob mulled it over, "We gotta get this ship out to the road and light it up."

I said, "When we going to do that?"

Bob responded, "Next weekend sounds good to me."

I agreed, "Let's do it. But look at that thing. No way can we lug this ourselves."

"Yeah," Bob's mind percolated, "We have to find a few trustworthy souls to give us a hand. And they can't be weenies, either. There are some neighbor kids I bet would be willing."

"Remember the code, Bob, mums the word."

We found a few not-so-ethical credible souls and set out on Sunday evening, October 3. 1965, to do our dirty.

Bob, I, and the troops gathered in the inky woods to transport the alien craft to its destination.

Bob gazed up, "I can't even see the stars; it's perfect. Everyone ready? Grab a leg."

"Bob, this saucer weighs a ton." The conspirators grumbled.

Bob grunted, "Alright, men, lift."

"Are you kidding me?" the donkeys mumbled.

Bob and I urged, "Come on, we can't be wimps. We can do this."

We muscled the fake glimmering "flying" machine through the woods and thick underbrush. Stumbling, tripping, and falling, trudging across the broad, uneven rutty field of tall grass. Like snakes in the pasture, not to be seen by possible traffic traveling the stretch of country road.

"We're here." Bob and I quietly said as we set the saucer in the center of Clinton Street.

I whispered, "Now turn on the rotary. Excellent. This is awesome-shiny, glittering, massive, and that red, amber, green spinning hanging light. Wow. This is going to freak somebody out for sure."

Bob proclaimed, "I see headlights coming. Everyone bolt!"

Bob and I ran but stopped halfway to the woods and hid in the tall grass. We surveyed the area but didn't see any of the colluders.

Bob whispered, "Guess they split through the woods and headed home. Weenies."

"Bob look, over there, those headlights turned off the highway; they're coming this way."

We watched as the car approached; we should have been wearing diapers.

Bob said, "Bummer, they are backing up to the highway."

Silence. Hearts beating.

"Bob, here comes another car; it's coming a little faster." They slammed on the brakes and made a U-turn. Then turned toward town.

"Whew, Bob, did you hear those tires squeal? Man, they laid down some rubber."

"Yeah, there're chickens."

About a half-hour went past, no traffic.

Then "Hey, Bob, on our right, here comes one over the hill. Whoa, he's bookin. He sees it. Think he's gonna hit it?"

The car quickly slowed to a crawl edging past the alien ship, two wheels on the pavement and two wheels in the weedy gravel.

Bob said, "There he goes. Bet he was scared shitless."

"Hey Bob, listen, you hear that? Its sirens. Take a gander over there toward town, red & blue lights coming our way. Oh man, the Fuzz are coming. I'm going to pee."

"Hang loose, Glenn, this is going to be good. Get low. They're getting out."

"Duck, I can't stand it." I quivered.

Bob replied, "you freakin' out?"

Flashlights were waving everywhere, and the cops were gathering.

I responded, "Here they come, head for the trees. No, wait. What are they doing? Aw man, they just shoved it over. Come on, let's go before they find us."

We turned tail and ran for the woods.

The Newburyport News and Amesbury News recorded the "historic" event.

October 3, 1965

This Saucer Was Grounded

Amesbury- It wasn't a flying saucer but it appeared to be one.

Police officers destroyed, Sunday night, what appeared to be a flying saucer on Clinton Street. However it turned out to be a prank.

A woman, whose identity was not disclosed came to the police station Sunday night and told officers, "There is something in the road in the middle of Clinton Street that looks like a flying saucer. It is about eight feet around and has three legs and is just standing there."

Flying Saucer Found A Hoax

AMESBURY- Amesbury police destroyed a "flying saucer" Saturday night. Officers John C. Holliday and David Frost were detailed to Clinton St. at 9:30 p.m. when reports came into the station that a "flying saucer" landed on the highway there.

The "saucer," made by Halloween pranksters, was eight feet high and ten feet around, stood on three legs and was covered with burlap and aluminum foil.

Holliday and Frost pushed the saucer-like roadblock to the side of the road and dismantled it.

ROADBLOCK in shape of a flying saucer on Clinton Street, Amesbury, Saturday night was broken up by police who said it was a burlap covered dome about 15 feet in diameter, standing on three aluminum covered legs eight feet high. The ruins were photographed Sunday near the R&G Mfg. plant.

About 40 years later, I was sitting at the dinner table shooting the bull with my brother-in-law Steve telling him about the flying saucer episode. Suddenly he stops me in the middle of the story.

"That was you?" Steve questioned. Steve's dad, Dusty, told Steve that a flying saucer landed near the "Flats." That is what we call the large field between the wood and Clinton Street. Steve's mom, Peggy, was home at the time. So when Steve didn't believe his dad, his mom piped up to support Dusty. Steve thought, oh my gosh, Mom never lies. I better go check this out. So pronto, Steve and his dad jumped in the car and ventured out to see the aliens. There were no seat belts in the '60s. Steve was standing on the back seat watching through the windshield when they cruised over the hill. Steve was disappointed at first. He was expecting helicopters, police, National Guard.... Dusty was speeding toward the long-legged broad Aluminum spacecraft. The landing light was spinning beneath the alien craft.

Dusty began yelling, "These aliens are not gonna get away." Steve became frightened, adrenaline pumping, thinking they might get zapped with a ray gun. Steve crashed to the floor. Dusty went off the road a bit and past the alien ship. Steve got up and peered out the back window- eyes of an owl. But then, realizing it was only a fake. When Steve told me his story, my grin turned to laughter. Mission accomplished!

FUGITIVE OR FLEDGLING

Two iron rods connected to an electrical cord, whose idea was that...? This is but one of our adolescent escapades.

In New Hampshire – whose motto is Live Free or Die – near the Massachusetts State Line from the dam, one can see the primitive Tuxbury Pond

Camp Ground, owned by Mr. and Mrs. Eaton. One way to get to the grassy, tree-lined, sandy shore is a canoe ride across the rippling pond and past the gnarly bushy uninhabited island. But the best way to get there is by the forest, navigating the narrow, winding, rutted dirt road through the semi-wilderness, then past the edge of the dry weedy meadow.

Barely past puberty, Bob and I contemplated getting out from under parental wings. But where, what? The idea came a little foggy at first, but then…. That would be awesome. A

month without the folks. Alone, by ourselves to do whatever, fend for ourselves. That's it, camping for a month.

I looked at Bob, "Ok, so let's ask our parents. Hey, wait.

How are we going to pay for this even if we can go? We got no jobs."

Bob responded, "We'll figure it out."

After a lengthy discussion, we convinced our parents to let us go. But permission came with a compromise and a condition, not a month, only two weeks. And we had to pay for the campout ourselves.

Bob, the brainiac, came up with the financial idea. "Let's sell worms to raise the money."

I asked, "Hmmm, how's that going to work? How do you get those crawly things, and how do we sell them?"

The idea came to mind; build a worm box bed. Next, get the worms, of course. Sometimes we dug, sometimes we poured soapy water on the ground - up they came. Also, we had fast hands, a bucket, a raincoat, and a flashlight on a rainy night. We captured dozens of juicy fat crawlers.

"Hey Bob," I said, "You know, I heard electric worm prods work."

Bob grinned, "Worm prods? Let's do it. Where do we get 'em?"

"I don't know, Bob. Let's make our own."

Bob shrugged, "But how?"

I countered, "We'll figure it out…. How about this? I got a pair of baby carriage axles. Yea. And an extension cord."

We cut one end off the extension cord and separated the

two wires. After removing the insulation, we threaded each bare wire through the holes of the thin rusty axles and wrapped the wire tight.

"Glenn, stick the rods in the ground, and I'll plug it in."

Bob calmly instructed.

I said, "Nah, go ahead, you do it."

"No, you can do it, Glenn."

I looked Bob in the eye, smirking. "Nah." - But then I pounded down the old iron rods.

Bob grabbed the plug and reached for the outlet. "Stand back. Here goes. It's in."

Nothing - no sparks - all the lights were still on. "Glenn, do you feel anything?"

"Nope, nothing," I said as I stood near the prods.

"Touch the ground, feel anything?"

I bent over and put my hand on the ground between the metal prods.

"Nope.", I trumpeted.

Bob yelled out, "Ok. Darn. Well, maybe the prods need to be closer together."

I murmured, "Ok, I'll move 'em," as I grabbed the metal rods. "Ahh, man, that hurts. Unplug it!"

"Right, you got it. Let's try 2 feet apart." Bob chuckled.

I moved the worm prods closer until I could feel the electrical tingling between them. The current commanded the worms to wiggle to the top of the turf.

The next idea was propagation. Those crawly things had lots of babies in the big worm box. The fishermen came one by one, dropping their moola into the cash can daily, week after week. We earned enough money to pay for our camp space and provisions. A glimpse of freedom, independence, fun in the sun, lose the leash.

A couple months later, we were on our way. We packed up and headed out. Bob and I set up a fantastic camp. Separated from other campers and several yards away from the mosquito-infested marshy and lily-padded shoreline. And close enough to the long-handled red pump with the note attached to a can."Please leave priming water." But we were not totally equipped for the mosquito war, ARGH.

We bathed in the pond. But whether bathing or swimming, we had uninvited guests, vampires that love nesting on young white flesh. The dark brown, flat, wide worms fed on our blood. But no worries getting those leeches off was easy. A little picking with the fingernail or shaking a little salt, no problem, they're gone.

The first few days in the forest by the pond were peaceful. We were enjoying our late morning Tuesday campfire. Until we saw the dust trail coming down the road, approaching the ragged field. We waited for the car to appear from under the dust veil, squinting and staring.

"Hey Bob, It's my mother's car." My hand shaded the sun from my eyes. "Crap, here come the moms."

"You've got to be kidding, our mothers?" Bob growled.

I responded, "What now?"

Bob kicked dirt on the fire. "Bolt, let's get out of here. Hide before they see us!"

I stood next to the smoldering coals, "What about the fire?"

As he ran toward the pond, Bob looked back, "Dump the coffee."

We split up and found cover.

Mom parked the car at our edge of the field, and the mothers began walking through the campground, searching, summoning.

"Bob, Glenn, hello... Glenn, Bob...."

I peeked from behind a distant tree. The moms descended on our private little camp, gazing at the smoke in the stone circle. My sister, Donna, brother, Ted, and dog, Princes, looked out the open car windows. The calling continued for twenty minutes. Then it happened. The mongrel got out. Canines have really great sniffers.... Imagine hiding from your mom and her desperately calling for you, then being found?

We tried to explain our desire to be by ourselves. I don't really remember exactly how that "conversation" went. But I recall mom doing most of the "talking," - not me. French women have a way of expressing themselves-body, soul, mind, and tongue. And mothers whose sons have just scared the bajibbies out of them for fear that some disaster may have taken over their sons. Like lionesses seeking a lost and endangered cub. After everyone calmed down, we gave profound apologies for their worries, sorrow, and hurt feelings. We were convincing enough to allow us to complete the remainder of our stay.

Moms have difficulty cutting the cord. But this eaglet already started branching, wing flapping, strengthening its muscles for life outside the nest.

IRVING III

Day two. I wonder if the search and rescue team will find him in time. Maybe it will become just a recovery effort....

The earth's natural satellite orbits the earth, 238,857 miles away. On a clear night, when the moon is like a large bright yellow cheese ball, my heart warms to look upon it. However, a godawful memory pierces my brain.

President John F. Kennedy, on September 12, 1962, announced to a large crowd at Rice University in Houston, Texas

"We choose to go to the moon."

It became a dream and a goal for the United States to be the first country to send a man to the moon and back. With this inspiration, our high school science club began its adventure in rocket flight. I was not part of the club but unexpectedly became involved at the school year's close.

In addition to the "spacecraft" building and launching came a unique project, live flight.

The class asked, "Who would we send? Who would volunteer?" It was like a government volunteer. You know, the young man that gets the letter from Uncle Sam.

"Greetings, your number has been selected. Report to the U.S. draft board."

Well, Irving III was selected. His training began immediately; time was running short. He was the perfect candidate, as his ancestry proved. Rugged, adaptable, and able to withstand rigorous testing. His physical size was suitable for the capsule, and his dark black fur coat offered warmth and protection for the flight. His keen sense of smell, sensitive ears, beady eyes, long whiskers, and tail did not provide any particular advantage. But neither did it pose any problems.

The time had come for the mighty mouse to undergo the rodent rocketeer training. The twirling, jolting, and maneuvers prepared Irving for this historic exploratory journey. Now nestled in his own specialized capsule, mounted on top of the cylinder of explosives, he was ready to zoom into the heavens. 10, 9, 8, 7…0 blast off.

I didn't witness the event, much to my disappointment. I only know of the excitement and success attributed to the science club through word of mouth. The rocket launch was successful, and all went well for Irving III. Except for two glitches.

First, they lost sight of the ballistic capsule shortly after launch. A search was immediately mounted; it took a couple of days to find where the capsule landed or, should I say, crashed. Tension and fear filled the heart of all who searched. Did Irving survive? Was he injured? Would he still be in the module? Finally, he was found. He was alive and well. Amazing!

Secondly, now what? The school year had come to an end. Torn from his family, he is now a hero but friendless and homeless. That's where I show up. The class desperately sought someone to take Irving in and make a dwelling place for him.

"I'll do it." I said, "I'll give him a home."

So the life of Irving III continued. It was a bit of a surprise for mom when I arrived home after school carrying a Mason quart jar ½ full of wood shavings, the top pierced with many holes. Inside was the cutest, spunkiest little fury black, beady-eyed, long-tailed creature. Even though Irving III had a new abode, his life was not without danger. Fun times with Irving were abundant, except on this particular tragic day.

My sister Donna and I were home alone. I gathered the family's thirty volumes of thick red encyclopedias and put them on the dining room table. No, not for instruction in human knowledge. He wasn't that kind of astronaut. I created a maze by stacking those large crimson hardbacks to test his ability and observe his behavior. I set Irving at the entrance of the complex arrangement. Knocking came at the front door. I called Donna to supervise Irving for a moment to make sure he didn't slip out of the maze while I went to see who was at the door. Wow, how life can change in a split second. Unbeknownst to Donna, lurking in the shadows was our furry striped cat. Tiger was scoping out his next meal. Hearing a melee, I turned around. Tiger leaped off the table with Irving clenched in his jaws.

It's been more than forty-nine years since this tragic day. Donna blamed herself for Irving III's demise. When we speak of Irving, she lowers her head, closes her eyes, and places her hand partially covering her forehead. But really, it wasn't her fault. I voiced my feelings of negligence. Neither knew that Tiger's cunning primal instincts would be exercised that day.

He lies in an unmarked grave at 138 Market Street, Amesbury, Massachusetts.

THE CHRISTMAS PARTY

High School Spring break. Henry, Howie, Bill, and I packed our sleeping bags and weekend gear into Henry's new 1964 Mustang and drove to the old three-room cabin on Rock Pond in the New Hampshire forest. We hid the booze in the trunk.

The snow had melted except for a few small patches in the shadows around Howie's dad's abandoned cabin. We cleaned out the mouse turds, scraped the dirt off the countertops, swept the tilted walls with the resident's ragged straw broom, flipped over the ancient urine-stained, smelly mattresses, and rolled out our sleeping bags. Darkness set in. We pulled out the hootch. Each a fifth to our liking. My choice was Gin (a distilled grain mash with juniper berries). I poured some firewater into the glass and filled the remainder with cranberry juice- I forgot the ice. I took my first sip of the Cranberry Slam cocktail, shuddered, and swallowed.

"Buha blaaa, this is nasty, tastes like pine needles." *Puke a rue- booze, this reminds me of the Christmas party.*

Flashback two years (a high school sophomore). I entered the banquet hall. The tables were set up in neat rows, decorated with candles, wreaths, and Christmas bulbs. The aroma of baked turkey, stuffing, sweet potatoes, and fixings blended with all the chatter and Christmas music: Sleigh Bells, Jingle Bell Rock, Santa Baby.... The managers, foreman, and employees of Saul Barbaro, the big old bald Jewish guy, were there.

The R&G metal cabinet factory is managed by Saul's meticulously groomed and educated son, John. Johnny's beautiful, well-maintained, finely equipped wife, Nancy, is also a vital part of the business. FYI (for your information), she bakes the best whoopee pies: white, creamy, vanilla frosting that oozes from between thin warm chocolate devil's food cake patties.

The Amesbury Chair Co. - once a part of R&G, where I work, is managed by Saul's son-in-law Dave and Saul's daughter Barbara. Barb wears a black bob-cut hairdo. The petite, cutesy, smiling lady would occasionally come out of the office and walk through the factory searching for Dave, exercising her natural bantam wiggle. No crevasse escaped the fragrance of Channel No.5. Production would stop. We, underlings, gawked. She was a jar of candy on a shelf out of reach.

I knew several of the Chair factory workers. Some were on probation, paroled, or hadn't been caught yet.

The "gentleman" of the Chair, Charley, a short, scrawny 80-year-old, is quite the crack-up. He liked to educate us working schoolboys about the ways of the world. The elderly guy told us about a pissing contest with his girlfriend.

Charley explained in his scratchy weak voice. "Me, Jack, and Mable were in the woods, and Jack had to piss. He said he could piss farther than me. I took the bet. Mable said she could outdo both of us. We dropped our drawers and began whizzing. Mable laid down, spread her legs, and took aim. Mable showed us both wrong." He raised his broom with both arms while chuckling as we listened in disbelief.

Orin, my line foreman, gives life lessons to us wet behind-the-ear boys. That's what he calls us, "wet behind the ears." He is a man of the world, experienced with women. He often boasts.

"I'll tell you what women really like," he carefully explained in sufficient detail, "the tongue, they really like the tongue…." His tongue mimicked the movements in between his instruction.

DISGUSTING!

Other wage earners also educate us schoolboys about the coarser things of life. At the party, Orin informed me that there was an open bar.

"What's an open bar," I asked.

The scraggly, crooked, yellow-toothed Orin grinned and looked at me with his small beady dark eyes.

"You can get whatever you want and don't have to pay for it. Coke, Pepsi, 7-up, Vodka, Whiskey, whatever. Don't worry. The bartender doesn't ask for ID."

The party went on; eating, drinking, loud chattering, music…. I asked the folk what they were drinking and got a small list: Whiskey and Coke, Margarita, Screwdriver, 7&7, Daiquiri, and Sombrero. I drank them all.

When I came out of the bathroom, my green face turned red. I was sure I wiped off the stuff on my shirt and chin. I leaned against the hall wall for support. Barbie doll passed by. When our eyes met, I knew I was busted. She smirked but said nothing.

The room quit swirling enough for me to find my seat. About an hour went by, and the spinning stopped. I went outside, clambered into my old '57 Plymouth, and drove home two miles. I got there at about 1 AM. As usual, the kitchen light was on. *Mom is up. She always stays up until I get home.*

Mom stood up as I passed through the front door and asked, "How was the Christmas banquet?" She observed my greenish complexion. Busted again.

I spoke on my way through the kitchen and up the stairs, "Oh, it was fine, you know, a lot of people, workers from the factory, bosses, and owners," I moaned and mumbled, "Going to bed now, tired."

She said nothing more, even the next day. I guess a greenish face was enough.

GYPSY LANE

The judge grasped the gavel with his right hand, locked his gaze upon the three of us, and said in a stern fatherly voice, "I don't ever want to see you, mischievous boys, in this courtroom again."

Bob, Al, and I all nodded respectfully in dismay. "Yes, sir."

He turned to the six hoodlums, "As for you delinquents..."

The judge ranted for several minutes without even a sentence delivered.

The gavel smacked down on the bench. "This court is adjourned."

"Wow," I said to Bob and Al, "I didn't see that coming. I thought we were the victims here."

All we wanted to do that boring starless night was a cruise through the willowwacks to the forbidden Gypsy lane. Then disturb whoever might be in the submarine races or playing kissy face. The fiasco started when Al shouted out the window, "Did you get any on you?" at the guy standing on the snowbank. Bob floored the "48" flat head 8 black Pontiac "Silver Streak." Flying over the twisted washboard gravel snow-patched lane.

Al hysterically repeated, "Bob, they are closing in fast."

The old bomber, the classic car that rode like you were on the living room sofa, was no match to outrun their muscle car.

All Bob's tricky maneuvers, cutting down side roads, turning off headlights, couldn't lose them. They were right on our tail.

I shouted to Bob, "Head for my place. We'll be safe there!"

Bob pulled up in front of my house. I cracked open the car door and then shut it quickly. The six drunk guys were pounding on the windows, fenders, and hood.

Bob screamed, "Oh shit." And stepped on the gas. We headed toward town. The drunkards were on our tail again, hanging out the windows, shaking their fists, and yelling obscenities.

After the third trip around Amesbury's town square, Bob pulled up in front of the brightly light old brick police station.

"Everybody out," Bob shouted.

Bob locked the car doors and took cover, waiting for help.

Al and I rushed up the steps of the police station as the delirious drunks pulled up right behind Bob's Pontiac. They jumped out of their car while screaming obscenities and running toward us like rabid dogs chasing chickens. Al and I burst into the Police station.

"They're going to get us. The thugs are crazy mad. Help, we need help!"

The thugs followed us into the police station. The officer in charge immediately rose from behind the desk and summoned help. The collision of Old Spice, English Leather, Jack Daniels, and donuts in the tiny lobby didn't deter the officer's duties. They restrained all eight of us. Then hastily barked out the command.

"Put your asses down on the bench." The men in blue handed us paper forms. Fill out your statements before I lock you up!" We peered through the open doorway and saw several available jail cells with black iron bars and bare wooden benches. We all chilled and completed our assignment. The charge officer ordered us to go home.

He said, "You will receive a summons to appear before the judge. He'll straighten out this matter of madness."

FOUR

WINGING IT

THE STRAWBERRY QUEEN AND A LETTER

Where is she now? It really doesn't matter. I have no control, no control at all, none.

Most of my belongings are packed in the trunk. As we head to Boston, I can see the Amesbury town square disappear through the rear window of dad's Pontiac. Wentworth Institute of Technology finally accepted my application after two years of trying to get in. The elite all-male Tech. School is a dream and goal of mine.

We survived the Boston city traffic and pulled up in front of the dormitory on Evans Drive. Dad helped me pack my stuff up to the second-floor room. We hugged and said our goodbyes; finally, emancipation!

I can almost reach each puke-green wall with my arms extended. One bunk bed, two closets, two desks, two electrical outlets & one window that overlooks buildings, concrete, and asphalt. Down the hall of Tuxbury Hall are the community bathroom and showers. The rooms across the drab hall view the busy street - a bicycle frame chained to a tree, the tires and wheels are gone, the seat gone, handlebars gone. Yep, just the frame and anti-theft chain are all that's left.

My second year is blessed with a few more "luxuries." Dominic and I survived the first year and decided to room together again. We live in Wentworth's Edward's Hall studio apartment on Huntington Ave. MBTA trolley tracks pass through the center of Huntington Avenue and head toward the Prudential Tower. A stone's throw away lies the fire station.

Frank walked into our room, soliciting, "My girlfriend, Mary Ann, has a college mate looking for a pen pal, is anyone interested?"

I haven't been going out with that California girl very long, like one month. I'm not sure where this relationship is going. I'll give this Pennsylvania chick a go and see what happens.

I said, "Frank, Dominic has a steady girl. But yeah, I'm in for that."

Frank responded, "I'll get the address for you; she's in a Pennsylvania nursing school. Her name is Linda Flynn."

September flew by, and December was halfway done. Prep for the semifinals is exhausting.

"Hey, Dominic, what are you doing for Christmas vacation?"

Dominic responded with a big cheerful grin, "I'm spending the whole two weeks with Paula. I'm not going with the old man on that lobster boat again."

"Well, I hope it goes better than last weekend. I thought you would get tired of all the bickering. You guys act like you're married. Well, you probably will marry her; you're about there anyway, just sayin, you know."

"Bullshit, Glenn. That will never happen."

"Hey Dominic, I'm headed to Pennsylvania for a few days to meet Linda, the nurse-to-be. I'm a little nervous, can't tell by a picture, but her writing is inviting. Time will tell."

The drive from Massachusetts to Pennsylvania and back went well. My vinyl is stacked on the spindle and one on the turn table, and I'm hitting the books. The semifinals are next week.

"Hey Dom, how was vacation?"

"Shitty, Glenn, shitty. We broke up. Think it's for good this time. Paula hosted the "Strawberry Queen." Bitch, bitch, bitch. Can't take it anymore. I'm done!"

"I don't think so, Dom, ha, ha, ha, you will marry this chick; just wait and see."

"How was your vacation?"

"Well, Dom, I had a good time, she is awesome and good-looking, but I don't know. I'm kinda messed up. It's been three months writing to Linda, taking the trip, and weekends with Cathy in Bean town. I can't do two. I have to choose."

"Dear Linda . . . hope we can still be friends, your pen pal, Glenn." I dropped the letter in the mail.

The week dragged on. I knew I had to come clean with the California girl. Confessions are really hard.

I wanted this relationship with Cathy to be good. But Linda, she is just so right; choices, ugh. Can't do two; maybe I won't even do one. Time will tell.

"Hey Cathy, I have a confession to make. On Christmas vacation, I took a trip to Pennsylvania with Bill. I met my pen pal friend . . ."

That conversation didn't go very well. Yelling and screaming and cursing. Then getting the cold shoulder for a few days.

Her confession came later. Georgia at grandmas was her Christmas destination, bonding with an old flame.

Days passed, the hurt between Cathy and me got buried, and our relationship continued. I never heard from Linda; we are not even friends; go figure. Where is she now? It really doesn't matter. I can't control what comes into my head. It really doesn't matter. The flame is dead.

THE BOOTH

I'm tucked away in the shadows between the rays of stained glass light from high above. Each Sunday, the parishioners sit and kneel for hours. My mahogany walls are dressed in hand-carved moldings and fancy metal trimmings. My seats and kneeling boards are hard, like the conversations inside me. I'm visited at scheduled periods during the week and listen to stories they tell, bearing their souls or not. Sometimes it is the same falsehoods, fulfilling their obligation; other times, it is gut-wrenching confessions. I have no voice, so they say what's on their mind and heart. Their whispers are captured like a dead man in a coffin covered with dirt. Only the man dressed in black with the white collar would be able to repeat what is heard, though he has taken a solemn confidentiality oath.

Father Johnson pulled back the curtain and took his seat on that scheduled late spring day. I watched as the dark-haired slender 20-year-old shuffled toward me. Ah, I recognize this guy. Yes, he is the young man I saw for the first time six Christmases ago and the one Christmas before that- he sat in the next to last pew, near the exit. Those are the only times I have seen him. Wow, he has come to visit me. Oh, I understand why he is here. Father Johnson encourages him, reinforcing the necessary step to a Catholic marriage. I listen as the young man confesses his sins. Father Johnson begins asking probing questions. The questions are not very intense but enough to prick his conscience. Softly the young man speaks. His body is relatively still, and the answers come quickly. Then the questions become more pointed as the man in black probes as if jabbing an armadillo, piercing the armor, going down the Ten Commandments list. The young man's answers come more slowly and in a quieter tone as he contemplates his responses. His head bends downward, his hands cover his face, and his voice quivers. His eyes water up as Father Johnson sits quietly, just listening to the confessions.

The husband to be answered, "Yes, stealing, fornication, lies...." Details from each violation are precise. No order of restitution comes from the hearer. The priest issues several prayers.

Finally, after a lengthy time, the young man pushes back the curtain and leaves me behind. His journey continues. He has come so near to meeting the One seeking him. So close but so far away. Confessions but no commitment of repentance. I'm just a booth, a portal. A place where people find temporary relief from burdens and guilt. I'm a quiet place to talk to the most vital One.

The marriage will occur as planned, but seeking the One who is pursuing him will go on.

THE GAMBLING MAN

John walked down the driveway to the post-mounted mailbox on the street, opened the mailbox door, slipped in several letters, and raised the red flag attached to the side.

He greeted me from across the street, standing six-foot-two, sandy brown, shortly cut hair. "Hey, Glenn, a beautiful day." He paused, looking me in the eye, "I get tired of writing "return to sender." These damn people keep sending me this stuff. Wish they would get it right."

He walked briskly toward me, sporting his sparkling hazel eyes and usual pearly white Cheshire smile. I met him in the middle of the street and returned the greeting with a hearty handshake.

John extended an invitation to me, "I'm going to Vegas this weekend. Would you like to come with Ellen and me?"

John's wife, five-foot-four, shiny brunette pixy cut hair, is a little firecracker.

I responded, "That sounds like a lot of fun, but I don't have any money..."

John interrupted, "You got twenty bucks? That's all you need. I'll pay for the plane fare, meals, and a three-night room at Cesar's Palace. Bring the wife. The craps tables are hot."

"That sounds great, John, but I don't know how to play craps."

"No problem, wait here. I have a twenty-page paperback,

It'll make you a winner."

John is the supervisor for Red Devil Fire Works in Fontana, California. He lived in a modest brown one-level three-bedroom stucco home in Rialto. The small front yard was framed by a split rail cedar fence, and the front lawn was decorated with two small palm trees and flora.

He made a deal with my brothers-in-law. They could swim any time if they cleaned and maintained the pool.

I lived across the street with the in-laws in a small one-story, three-bedroom, blue-green stucco house with my wife and her brothers; Joe, Mike, Larry, John, Gerry, her twin step-sisters Lisa and Dee. I had just turned twenty-one; my wife, the chameleon nineteen-year-old, had snagged me from my lifelong dreams of being an architect. I drove our two-door Plum crazy purple Volkswagon from Amesbury, Massachusetts, to Rialto, California. We stuffed belongings into the car. The overflow went into the hand-crafted black wood roof rack, except for what a young man leaves behind with mom and dad.

I studied the book, took the plane, and the luxuries at Caesar's Palace. The chameleon hid in her room. Late that evening, I hit the tobacco-hazed craps venue, ignoring the breast-popping blouses and short red-skirted damsels carrying free booze trays.

I put to use my newfound knowledge of how to play craps. Seven come eleven points in-between, and an occasional Field bet. I doubled my bet after every time the die bounced wrong. Rolling the pair on the green felt was lucrative. The twenty dollars turned into a hundred, five hundred, and fifteen hundred… I stuck five-hundred bucks into my shoe, called it a night, and hit the sack. Well, actually, morning. It was three AM. Later in the day, after steak and eggs, I paid John for the room, plane fare, and food. Back to the craps table. It didn't go well. The pair became a thief and took all my cash. Except for my soul money, which I returned home with.

Several months later, I saw John walk down his driveway to the post-mounted mailbox on the street. He opened the mailbox door and stuffed in it several white envelopes, and raised the red flag attached to the side.

I greeted him from the in-laws' front lawn across the street where I still lived with the chameleon wife.

"Hey, John, nice day. What's up?"

I stood on the front lawn as he shuffled across the street to meet me. His lips were pressed tight, and his head hung low.

"I have to leave town," he said.

"Where you going, John?"

"Far from here, I don't know. Maybe Michigan. The FBI, FBI.

They're coming. They caught me marking "deceased" on the bills I've been putting back in the mailbox. Say, do you want to buy my house? Well, not purchase, just take over payments. I'll go to the courthouse with you and sign the papers. I must get out of here by the end of the week."

The chameleon wife and I became owners of the modest single-level stucco house. And the swimming pool. My brother-in-law Joe taught me to swim. I honored John's agreement with the boys. They clean and can swim any time. We had many days of cooling off from the scorching southern California sun.

In November, a friend from back east, Mary, and Al, her new beau, appeared at our front door. They visited for a few days. One evening the four of us were sitting at the bar in our bright lime-green and white kitchen with the indoor-outdoor blue and green checker carpet.

Al piped up, "Who dares to swim naked?"

Mary and I headed to the pool under the starlit sky. But the chameleon wife and Al started clucking and showed feathers.

Since then, I have gone to Vegas several times but stuck to the one-arm nickel machines.

NEVER AGAIN

The telephone rang. On the other end was a weak, quivering, and desperate voice.

"Mom, I need a ride. I've been puking for three days and haven't eaten. Bad stomach pains, I can barely stand."

"Joe, you sound terrible. Where the hell have you been?"

"I'm up here at Grants Pass, Oregon. The commune thing is not working."

"I could wire you some bus money."

"Don't think that will work. I don't have transportation and can't wait that long."

"I'll find someone to come to get you. They could be there tomorrow evening. Joe, Call me back in a couple hours."

"Damn, mom, hurry. I'll let you know the spot where they can find me."

My brother-in-law, Joe, was a slender, blond long-haired, adventurous dude, 4 years my junior. I was 20. I moved from Massachusetts to Rialto, California, three months ago. Geraldine or Gerry, Joe's mom, recruited me for the 767-mile drive to rescue Joe from his hippie experience. This created a special bond between Joe and me. The following is a story of one of our adventures several decades later in Idaho

The old Jeep Cherokee Wagoneer was loaded with camp gear, a canoe, and a tepee. We traveled on Hwy.75; miles of sagebrush was in the rearview mirror. A lava rock lunar landscape passed by the side window as we headed for our annual Memorial Day camp-out. As we descended Timmerman hill into the valley, the distant mountain peaks of the Sawtooths came into view. A beautiful view of white caps and rugged terrain lay before us. Our excitement grew as we could almost taste the adventure that lay ahead. Just another hour or so, and we would be at the lakeside. Bellevue, Ketchum, and Sun Valley were soon behind us. The pavement was no longer straight, and the Cherokee strained to make the grade. Galena summit was covered with snow, the banks rose above the Jeep, and the pine tips decorated the virgin pure white cover. We totally did not expect such an accumulation of white stuff.

The smell of the burning brake pads and the grinding sound of the metal drums filled the Cherokee cab as we dropped into the valley. Patches of snow and ice-covered Highway 75 as we squinted toward the noon sun, zigzagging closer to our planned destination. Finally, ahead of us, as we rounded the corner, barely above the snow, pasted on a dark brown board in white letters, "Lake Alturas 3 miles".

"Awesome, Joe, this is it. Turn here, just a few more miles."

"At last. Hey, Glenn, the snow isn't completely covering the ground. Wait, the gate is closed. What's that say? No way, 'campground closed,' Glenn, tell me I'm wrong."

"You're kidding me. Closed? Joe, I didn't come all this way just to go back. I think you can go around the gate. Put it in four-wheel."

"Hey, man, let's do it. I think I can buck through that drift."

Joe stepped on the gas.

"High-centered, Joe, we are high-centered. Stuck, we're not going anywhere and have no soul in sight."

Joe responded. "Well, this is it. We're here. We're pretty close to the lake. Let's unload the stuff, Glenn, and set up camp."

We pulled the 20-foot poles off the top of the brown and white Cherokee and set 3 to the side. Joe lashed the tops together, and we stood up the tripod as a foundation to complete the erection of the tepee canvas and the other poles, numbering about 14 poles altogether. After the outer shell was fitted, we attached the inner liner, gathered firewood, and finished setting up camp.

The stars popped out through the tops of the trees and across the partially frozen lake until nearly the entire sky was blanketed. The moon cast shadows across the landscape. Alone, deafening silence, the scent of fresh pines, the unblemished patches of snow, the undeniable presence of God and His creation. We soaked it all in before climbing into our sleeping bags nestled close to the campfire's warmth in the center of the tepee.

The sun rose, and our day's adventure began as we unloaded the canoe off the top of the snowbound Cherokee, wondering how we would get out of the drift. No worries, enjoy the day. The canoe slid into the icy, clear water. We carefully navigated through the vast large chunks of ice that filled the pristine lake. The only sound was the canoe and icy water slapping together, interrupted by our occasional conversation and laughter. Never again would this happen, this solitude (though somewhat unlawful) and this particular beauty be enjoyed.

Day 3 was totally different. The Forest Service decided to open up the campground. Not too long after breakfast, we heard the sound of voices, at a distance at first, then closer and more plenteous. Yes, the city has come to the wilderness. But what a blessing. We were ready to pack up and call our adventure journey to an end anyway. Just one more thing, The Jeep Cherokee was still snowbound. Praise God, the voices had arms and legs, muscular arms and legs. We were soon out of the drift and on our way home. Adventures like these only happen once in a lifetime, for me, anyway. I've been to Lake Alturas many times since 1979. It's not the same.

THE KEYS

April said, "Hey Megan, that was a fun cruise."

"Yeah, it sure was," Megan replied

"Meg, motor me to the Pit Stop, so I can drive Pinky home before curfew."

"You got it, girl.'Blame It on The Rain' that's an awesome tune. Milli Vanilli are so rad. We'll be there in a minute."

"April, where's Pinky? I don't see Pinky! Didn't you park her right in front?"

"Megan! Where is she? What the… she's not here!"

Oh, little city of Wendell, how still we see thee lie. Just before the setting sun, a lesson has just begun.

The Smothers Brothers show just ended. I got my lazy butt off the couch, climbed into the 1977 family two-tone brown four-door Chevy Caprice Classic, and headed to Simerly's Grocery and Sporting Goods. I drove the short 5 blocks and stopped at the octagonal red sign. The east breeze carried the usual pungent dairy barn odor across town. Over my right shoulder, strung across Idaho Street, supported by the large vertical I beams, is the gallantly displayed huge vintage Wendell, Hub City Sign. Looking over my left shoulder. I caught a glimpse of that treasured Mary Kay Pink Bug. *Hmmm, wonder why she's parked there?* I quickly made a left turn and pulled up in the parking lot. I strutted to the side of the car and peered through the gray-tinted window. I couldn't see much, so I tugged on the chrome door handle. *Hmmm, unlocked.* As I opened the door, the sweet fragrance of vanilla drifted past me. Everything about the black refurbished interior was in order. April's boom box (temporary stereo system) rested on the seat. Then my eyes caught sight of what I was afraid of. Yep, dangling from the ignition was the fancy key ring. *I can't believe she did it again. How many times have I told her?*

Grrrr. Don't leave your keys in the car. I jumped back into the brown bomber and headed home. *Forget the groceries.*

She's getting three bucks an hour, working at the Wendell Mall Pharmacy, not sure how many years it takes to pay for this dream.

I pulled up into the driveway and went into the house. "Hey Aaron, come with me. I need your help. I need a driver."

"What's up, dad?"

"Your sister left her keys in the car again, parked the "Pepto Bismol" thing in front of the Pit Stop, and must have gone to Twin with Megan. She just can't remember keys, keys, girrrrurl."

We got into the four-door "luxury" sedan with brown cloth seats and McDonald's French fry aroma. I glanced over at Aaron and saw a little twinkle in his eye. *Ah, I wonder what is going through his head. He looks pretty excited.* I drove to the Pit Stop alongside the 72 dream mobile. We decided to hide her car and take the keys. I climbed into the Bug and turned the key. That familiar wingding, ding sound roared from under the rear hood, beep-beep. I drove Pinky up behind Leslie Welding, well out of sight. Aaron followed me in the Caprice.

I said, "We better get home. April's curfew will be here soon."

"Hey, dad, this is awesome. She is gonna be, well, you know...."

Aaron and I sat in the living room and waited for it to all comedown. The door burst open. April began her rant with tears and sobbing.

"My car, my car...."

Aaron couldn't help himself, splitting a gut laughing. April responded with some "sisterly love." I stood there till April emptied herself. Before handing over the keys, I shared the plot and gave the fatherly key sermon. Again.

"Hey, April, let's go get your car."

I talked to April on her cell phone years later and asked her, "Do you leave your keys in the car?"

My Master Degree daughter responded, "No, dad, I always take my keys out and lock the door."

FIVE

MISHAPS AND ILLUMINATIONS

THE RIGHT SIDE

Times of Learning and Pain

Bill said, "Don't run. He won't bother us. We'll be O.K."

The only thing separating the young steer from the five strands of tightly strung barbwire was us. We were on the wrong side of the fence. But not in the bovine's eyes. I glanced up the sloped pasture and saw the castrated bull lift its head, twitch his tail and turn his body downhill. Bill, the country boy, and I continued walking, but now the steer had our full attention. The white-chested horned critter took a few slow steps toward us. Then into a trot. Bill was several yards ahead of me. Closer to the end of the clumpy field. Easy access to escape. So he ran.

I yelled, "Thought you said not to run!" I began to walk more briskly. The yearling must have said to himself, "It's playtime." I ran. It ran faster. Faster than a ten-year-old city boy could run. His horns were like parentheses around my ribs. His weight pushed this trespasser through the sharply pointed pieces of twisted rusty wire. I was wounded.

There is a bruise between my shoulder blades. And a white crescent scar below my ring finger on my right palm. Evidence of the torn flesh.

When I was twelve, Wayne McFadden and I built a fort in the woods. We chopped down several small pine trees with our hatchets. I hummed "Battle of New Orleans" and danced while using my new leather-handled razor-edged steel hacker. Wayne was doing a fine job erecting the future hide-out.

Then it happened. I call it a rubber tree. I swung my hatchet at its base. The antagonist deflected the short-handled ax into my right shin and laid it open. I waited for the blood to come. *What, no blood?* I dropped the hatchet and pulled my pant leg up. Wayne and I stared at the flapped skin for a moment. Laughter didn't seem appropriate, but that's what we did. I lifted and curled back the chunk of loose flesh. All that was visible were dozens of tiny red dots where the hatchet sliced my leg nearly to the bone.

On the right side, slightly above my ankle, I bear the proof with the ugly scar on my shin.

In the late summer of 1978. A year and a half after my Idaho arrival. My family piled into the ex-Californian in-laws' Ford Econo van and trekked to the Trinity Lakes campground. The only amenity of this high mountain wooded basin is a fire pit of smooth granite river rock.

I grabbed the ax while the others were setting up tents and preparing camp. I had a little experience with an ax, so I thought it fitting to cut some firewood. I stood up one of the fat short log rounds the previous campers left to split it with the ax. I held the long handle tightly and raised the ax to take a mighty swing. The ax sunk deep into the log, but it didn't split. I raised the ax again. The chunk of wood didn't come free. I banged it against the ground several times to loosen it from the ax but to no avail. Then I stood over the embedded ax and gripped the handle close to the head. I gave a hardy tug. The heavy pine mass was co-joined with the ax - only for a split second. The ax came free of the log. It was too late for me to move away from the trajectory of the blunt steel end of the treasonist. The speedy flat iron hit me square on the nose. There was blood. An open wound.

Today, if you look at me intently between the eyes, you will see a sign, a clue, on my nose. More in the center than on the right side.

These two injuries remind me of more tales to tell. More scars, most of them self-inflicted, negligence on my part.

When I lived on C Street in Wendell, Idaho, in the late 80s, a west gale blew down one side of our six-foot cedar fence. And half the roof shingles. My homeowner's insurance covered the repair of the privacy wall and some roof repair costs. The roof shingles were aged enough that a total replacement was needed. I didn't have the money to replace the roof. But my good friend, Gary Phelps, knew of my dilemma and lent me the money. He was kind enough to say not to worry about paying back. Whenever I had the money, I could pay him the $500. He also helped me install some of the new shingles.

At the end of the week, I was finishing the roof. Only the trimmed shingles on the peak of the house remained to be installed. I perched myself in the driveway on a gray plastic Falconhust Dairy milk crate. I sat in the shade of the roof overhang in front of the garage door and stacked shingles on my lap to cut several three-tab shingles into the ridge cap pieces. The last asphalt shingle lay on the right leg of my 501 button-fly Levi jeans. I heard a small still voice in my head.

"Glenn, this is not very smart. Stop. Don't do it." I'm not very good at taking advice. My brain does not quickly communicate information to the rest of my body.

The knife sliced through the thin black asphalt, blue jeans, and skin like a scalpel through a watermelon.

I said to the voice in my head. "Oh no, damn…."

The sharp metal parted the flesh on the inside of my right side knee.

I yelled, "You idiot!"

I scampered into the house and pulled down my pants. Crap. *If I go to the hospital, they'll probably give me a tetanus shot and stitch me up. That will take time. I have to finish the roof.* I scrubbed the wound with soap and water and grabbed the blue bottle of ST 37 disinfectant applied to the injury. Then slapped on a couple Band-Aids. This slowed the bleeding. I pulled up the 501s and went back to work.

The one-inch scar reminds me to consider the advice and be careful with a utility knife.

One decade and a few years later, it happened. I hope it's the last time to be on the right side. I finished helping to mow Mrs. Wimberley's yard and pushed my lawnmower to the back of my pick-up. I dropped the tailgate and grabbed the bottom of the mower with both hands to lift it into the bed. There was a quick sizzle of burning flesh. The underside of my right wrist was pressed firmly against the muffler. I let go of the beast, then quickly ran to the cab of my truck and opened the jockey box. I poured the soothing Melaleuca T36-C5 oil on the wound. This brought temporary relief, but the ache and burn took several months to heal. The discolored and uneven skin patch reminds me of my mother's childhood warning. "Glenn, don't touch. It's hot."

RETURNING TO IDAHO

In June 1970, my Seventeen-year-old wife and I visited Mountain Home to see her uncle, stationed at the airbase. Our drive from Massachusetts across the northern United States had been fascinating until we entered southern Idaho. This twenty-year-old Yankee boy had never seen such a hellish place.

The scorching sun was uninhibited, and it torched the flesh. The sea of sage-brush and sandy dirt had no horizon. And the shade. What shade?

We went to the only place above the flat land, the Bruneau Dunes. The sand burned my feet. It stuck to my wet skin, and my vision was obscured by the blinding sun and salty sweat. I struggled to the top of the dune with my cardboard "sled," which did not work. I walked and rolled all the way down the hill. We went back to her uncle's house for lemonade and to cool off.

"This has to be the armpit of the nation," I told myself and numerous others. "Who in their right mind would ever want to live here?"

The next day, we were on the road again, headed to California, where Cathy's parents lived. We settled there for four years before returning to Amesbury, Massachusetts. I was happy to be back amid the warm summer days, where the grass was beautiful shades of green, and an abundance of oaks, maples, and elms provided lots of shade. The hills, lakes, and streams were a joy to my soul. The occasional Atlantic breeze was refreshing.

Three years later, we got a call from my mother-in-law.

"We moved to Idaho. We want you to move out here and join us."

"Are there any trees out there?" I asked. "Because I don't remember seeing any."

"Oh yes," she responded. "Filer is different than Mountain Home. There are a lot of trees here."

"Is there any water? Any hills?"

"You should come, it's really nice. And way different than California. The people here are friendly, the air is clean, and it's not crowded."

The in-laws were persuasive, so I sucked it up and started packing. A moving truck was too expensive to rent for the one-way trip to Filer, so we bought an old GMC red-and-white, sixteen-foot box delivery truck fitted with a pull-out ramp and an extra gas tank. The sellers purchased the six-wheel hauler in Florida to move to Massachusetts. I planned on selling the dinosaur once we got to Filer.

We loaded the rig up on a Saturday to leave early Sunday morning. I put our eldest daughter, April, seven, into the cab along with her cat, Christy Prince. John, my brother-in-law, was waiting for us at the side of the road. He had flown to Massachusetts to drive our blue Datsun coupe with my wife, five-year-old son, Aaron, and Lori, our four-month-old daughter. I cranked down the window and said goodbye to my parents.

I released the emergency brake, pressed on the gas, let out the clutch, and began nudging out of the driveway onto Highway 150. April scooted to the front edge of the worn and torn cloth

bench seat and braced herself against the metal dashboard. She peered through the windshield while the cat howled and meowed and ran back and forth across the top of the seat.

"Car coming, Dad."

The brake pedal went to the floor to little effect. I quickly pulled up the emergency brake lever. We went nowhere that day. Dad and I replaced the master brake cylinder a couple days later after the part came in.

Once again, off we went on our seven-day journey across the northern United States. When we arrived at the in-laws' place in Filer, I turned a corner into the gravel driveway and stepped on the brake pedal.

"Oh, no, not again."

The in-laws had a large yard. I rolled to a stop.

Several months later, after I repaired the brakes, I sold the truck to our friends, Steve and Ann, who were moving to Texas. Their trip went well, except for a minor setback in replacing a blown engine in Colorado. When they got to Texas, they sold the gas-guzzling beast to people moving to the Southeast.

Returning to Idaho turned out to be a good thing. I've now been here for more than forty-three years. I like the sagebrush, even though I still find the shades of brown hard to get used to.

I like the people, except some of the newbies.

"That's not how we do it in California," the newbies now say to me. "You can do that here?" Or they say, "Really, you don't have that here?"

If you don't like it, don't try to change it. Go back to where you were happy.

"Watch out for the ticks and rattlesnakes," I tell them.

I like the endless sky, the Sawtooth Range, the caves, and the canyons. The wide-open spaces. Here in the Magic Valley, the wind always blows. I don't like that, except in the summer, it feels good. The liberties here are nourishment to the mind and heart.

GOOD RIDDANCE

I put her on the bus
Suitcase in her hand
No kiss goodbye
I tried not to cry

From Idaho to Carolina
The excuse is her ailing dad
Time told that was a lie
Her arrival was a surprise

Excuses came and went
No commitment was her bent
Her doubted return was evident
Care for me is all I can do

My life on hold would never work
Don't know why she is such a jerk
Wouldn't come home for family or me
So the lawyer's letter I sent

Two months later came relief
The judge pronounced my release
I prayed to God for a new wife
Someone to love and cherish

The prayer came true God provided
She's beautiful, glorious, a friend, a companion
A soulmate to the end.
And loves the Lord, no doubt

Good riddance
Good luck, men-to-be
She mounted her broom
Found another groom, or two or three.

FACING THE VOID

Torment. Turmoil inside me. Betrayed. I'm trying to identify feelings. It's like trying to find, well, I don't know.... I've buried my emotions for so long that I can't remember if I've ever had feelings. This is going nowhere.

Betrayal didn't come like a Venus flytrap snatching a fly. It was more like the oxygen being sucked out of the air a little bit at a time until I realized I couldn't breathe anymore. It began with frustration. The coldness of the wife's physical contact. Minor at first, then increasing slowly as time went on. The lack of sexual intimacy followed in increasing measures. Sometimes several months without any sex. Then there were the times of absence from home.

Like, "Glenn, I need to stay with Betty's mom in Twin Falls. She's not doing well and needs help."

I replied, "O.K. Cathy, do you know how long you'll be there?"

"I'm not sure," she responded.

"Well, will you let me know?"

"I'm not sure. I'll be in touch sometime."

Communication became torturous. Every discussion went circular. Our discussions of problems and issues eventually came to be my fault. My frustration turned to punch holes in doors. Five holey doors. Each one happened on a particular day, weeks apart.

Twenty-seven years later, I sit here at McDonalds", finding my solitude in the crowd's noise. Digging up the past. I would rather bury it and put a tombstone on it. I keep grasping for the deeply hidden feelings, but it's like wandering through the fog, trying to catch a cloud.

Betrayal that sneaks up on you sucks. Marriage undone, one thread at a time. At least to this oblivious man.

Thinking back, more significant events began to take place. Abandonment, yep, I put the frigid woman on the Gray Hound with no definite plans to return. This time it was her dad in North Carolina. She said he was not doing well and needed help.

Several weeks passed, and I had no solid answers about her return. I made a more determined phone call.

"Hello, Cathy, how's it going?"

"Oh, Glenn, it's going good. Dad's better. I've got my own place now."

"What do you mean you've got your own place?"

"Yeah, I've got my own place and a job at Olan Mills Photography."

"You what?"

"I'm happy. I'm renting a trailer in the park and have a full-time job."

"Well, when are you coming back home?"

She replied, "Home?"

"Yeah, home. When are you coming home?"

"I don't know, Glenn. I'm not sure."

"O.K., well, you go ahead. Do what you want. But I'm not putting my life on hold. I can't get any straight answer from you, so I'm also going ahead with my life."

"What do you mean?"

"I mean, I'm going on with my life. Call me when you get things figured out. But I'm not waiting. If you want to be part of my life, come home."

I woke up to loneliness night after night. Loneliness turned to more frustration and, what else, anger? Lost at sea, every day searching for land. Tears, loneliness, frustration, exasperation.

Her departure was brutal because she told me that divorce was never an option before we got married. She grew up in a divorced home and experienced several stepmoms. She did not want that for her family. But here I was, betrayed.

Several months before her first departure to help Betty's mother, I was upset with our marriage relationship. In the shower, I became angry, looking for some solution. I decided that my relationship with God was the problem. I had been accused many times of being too religious. I prayed, "God leave me alone, get out of my life. You're wrecking my marriage."

Betrayal, had I betrayed God? As time progressed, nothing in the marriage relationship changed. I realized my God abandonment prayer was not the solution. After several months, I prayed for forgiveness and decided to pursue my relationship with God more deeply.

Did my divorce betray my children? This question surfaces occasionally. Should I have endured the painful cold-hearted adulteress wife for the sake of the four children, hoping for a change of heart from the betrayer?

Did I betray our family? Was my selfish ambition in looking for a soulmate, someone to love and care for, a betrayal to my children? The now ex-wife betrayed and abandoned the four children and me. Who does that?!

Feelings, ugh. Women identify and talk about feelings all the time. Not guy talk, like grunts, groans, and nods. Feeling thing is hard. I don't like it. Keep digging.

Hurt, anger, frustration, sorrow, revenge, no, not revenge. Love.

I'm afraid to talk to the kids. Do the boys have the same issue as I do? That is with feelings? What about the girls? They may become unleashed. Could I handle it? Well, just the eldest daughter, April. My Lori passed away in 2014. I'll never know her struggle.

The void has been filled. My wife of 25 years, Linda, is incredible. On the other hand, the ex has gone through more than three husbands. The third one died.

BUSTED

During their close-out sale in Twin Falls, Linda and I loaded up the barbeque we bought from Ernst Home Center. It was a wedding gift for my oldest son, Aaron, age twenty-two, and his bride, Michelle. The sun was setting as we drove from Twin Falls to Jerome. We crossed the Perrine bridge and turned west onto Golf Course Road. Before the curve passed the golf course, we turned north again, taking a back road for a shortcut to Aaron's and Michelle's place. They were renting from Aaron's mother, my ex-wife.

I was not allowed on the property because of the restraining order I filed against her. The judge declared that we were not permitted to be on or near each other's property. Aaron said to come anyway; she lived in Winnemucca and wouldn't know.

We approached the double-wide Mobile Home with the scruffy yard on 400 South Road. We pulled over at the entrance to their gravel driveway on the wrong side of the road, facing oncoming traffic. The chain-link fence gate was open, an ideal place to unload the large two-burner hooded black metal grill. I left the pick-up engine running with the headlights on. Linda stayed in the cab while I went to open the S 15's tailgate. Just as I got to the back of the truck, I saw a vehicle turn onto 400 South Road, about a quarter-mile away, heading toward me. Their headlights flashed from low to high beam several times quickly. The compact pick-up raced toward me, continuing to flash its lights. The vehicle eased along the edge of the pavement with two wheels almost in the burrow pit. He slammed on his brakes, stopped several yards from the front of my truck, and flung open the driver's door. The fat short guy walked briskly toward me, yelling obscenities. Waving his arms and shaking his fist. I could smell the booze as he got closer. He stood before me by my tailgate in the glare of headlights. Glazed, bulging eyes pierced through any security I had.

"Turn off your headlights. Turn the fucking damn things off. Now. Turn them off!"

I responded, "I will, just a second. As soon as I unload."

"No, you asshole, off now, or I'll bust your fucking headlights out. Now you asshole. My daughter wrecked from fuckers like you. Turn them off."

He was in my face, all three hundred pounds of him.

"O.K." I muddled. I started walking toward my cab.

He turned around, jogged back to his work truck, and pulled out a three-foot iron crowbar. The Rhino lowered his head and began charging toward my ride. Hearing the commotion, Linda reached over and turned off the headlights. The grimy thick-skinned, short-legged mammoth raised the long bar of destruction as he loped toward the front of my truck.

"Too late, fuck it. Asshole. Your damn fucking headlights are gone."

He stood in front of my pick-up. With two swift blows, he smashed out both headlights, turned around, and strolled back to his truck, leaving me in a stench of redneck soda. He slid into his bantam orange pick-up. Slammed the door, laid some rubber, and disappeared down the road.

I left the BBQ on the tailgate, got into the truck, grabbed the bag phone, and called the Jerome County Sheriff.

"I'm here at 29 East 400 South Road. Some guy just busted out my headlights…." After what seemed an eternity, the Deputy arrived.

The inquisition started, "What happened? Can you describe him? Did you get the vehicle plate number? Description of the truck? What time did it happen…?"

"Can you go after the guy, Officer?"

The Deputy responded, "No, not enough vehicle description, and he is long gone. But I could write you a citation for parking on the wrong side of the road."

The beast got away, and I escaped being busted. Two slain headlights and nearly crapping my pants were enough punishment.

Aaron was fuming, but it all happened before he could get off the front porch. He met me at the tailgate. We unloaded the wedding gift and hugged. Linda and I borrowed Aaron's car to go back home to Wendell. *Is it illegal to drive in the moonlight with no headlights?*

WHAT'S A NAME

Some Senior Thoughts and Ramblings

I wish he would die! The memory is hidden in a dense fog. I think his name was Robert Gamblin, and I don't know if any of my former Junior High class-mates remember him. He used to tease, torment, and bully me. One time I went to his place after school. His house needed paint, some windows were broken, and the roof was missing shingles. The long dirt-rutted driveway was partially weed-covered. The odor of pigs drifted across the property. There was an eerie stillness about the place. The day's happenings escape my memory. Robert died shortly after that day. The rumor was that he fell into the silo and could not get out. My stomach still turns, and my heart is troubled every time I remember my wish coming true. Robert did not have a nickname.

Friends and family have nicknames. Billy, real name, William. Robert is Bob; it was Gene, not Eugene. For Wilfred, my dad, Willie, sometimes called Junior, common shortenings of the day. Al for Albert, his sisters are Tootie and Toolie. These gracious names call up feelings, like embracing a bouquet of wildflowers or sipping well-aged whiskey. I didn't know their real names until the end of High School year's end.

My cognomen came at age 28 when I worked at Amesbury Specialty Inc., a metal fabrication factory. The title was bellowed daily and ricocheted off the shipping department walls like a "Squash" game. Pee Wee, Pee Wee. It smelled like Skunk spray. The designation never left my lips or was put on paper until this present writing. It's been forty-three years. Who knows why they picked that name. I say them. Because it took a number of those numb skulls, including Birdie, to think of such a dingbat name. His handle matched the size of his brain. I never did figure out his actual name. But, Pee Wee? Come 'on. What enchanted forest or glorious valley is called Pee Wee?

What's in a name anyway? Glenn Paul Theberge, now that's a name. Mom says a legend was born on that day.

How will I be recognized? Will it be from the engraving on my head-stone? No. How do I remember a name: Did he work three jobs to support his family, or did he spend his welfare check sitting on the couch eating chips and drinking soda? Does he mow his frail, aging neighbor's lawn for free? Or does he accept money for doing her repairs? Did she take communion on Sunday morning and stab her friend in the back on Wednesday? Did she abandon her husband and family to pursue her own happiness? Or did she nurture her step-children as her own? That's how I remember a character.

It's a bizarre world. Sometimes a name is just wrong. When I was ten, my neighbor friends and I would play army outside. Their brother stayed in his bedroom performing Barbie dress-up. His name should have been Alice. As an adult, he married Frank.

My niece married a big strapping guy, as described to me, who wears skirts and has boobs. Patrick's new name is Patty. I still can't get my head around that one.

In the latest debacle, my ex-son-in-law is now bent. The fellow is no longer straight. He ditched my daughter and is turned on by guys. What should his name be?

What's in a name-Lord have mercy...

LOST AND CONFUSED

Age 70 is not the only cause for being occasionally lost or confused. In my younger years, this state of mind was present several times. My wife says that my IQ is OK. My mother would say the same. But I'm not sure I know about being lost or confused; these are two past recollections of my condition.

Meeting at the apartments.

I can't believe I'm sharing this most embarrassing story. I might have a rare condition. I don't have a severe case, but I'll blame this incident on Prosopagnosia, face blindness.

Several months had gone by since I had seen Aaron. He called to invite me to meet him at the apartment he was renting in Boise. The occasion was to visit my oldest son, bring him a cat's paw, a tool for pulling nails, and meet his girlfriend, Michelle.

Linda and I fueled up the little blue 1988 S15 pickup truck. Dad's low-mileage spotless gift to me that I drove to Idaho from Massachusetts, with the $1.15 a gallon unleaded regular at the Maverick before leaving the "Hub City." Wendell's nickname. I call it nothing in the middle of everything. It's an excellent location for wherever a person may want to go. Really, it is a friendly small city. We left town using the west exit to get on the "super slab." The 100 miles plus drive, nearly two hours of sagebrush viewed out the side window, and an occasional tumbleweed smashing into the grill at the new speed limit of 65 miles per hour. For several years it was 55 MPH due to the oil embargo.

We got to the apartment complex by mid-afternoon. I wasn't sure exactly where to meet Aaron. He just said meet me in the parking lot. I pulled into the vast parking lot and looked for a place to park. Finally, I found a spot in the congested lot. Linda and I sat in the pickup quite past the appointed meeting time. I became impatient and decided to leave the truck and walk to the apartments. Maybe I could find his name on a mailbox and wait for him at the apartment. A pickup truck was slowly rolling by on my way across the pavement. I waved for it to stop. The passenger lowered the window and began a conversation with me. He had a kind of smirk on his scruffy, dirty-whiskered face. After we had talked for a few minutes, a strange feeling began to overcome me.

The "stranger" said, "Dad, I'll meet you at 24 C."

I said, "OK, see you in a minute."

Wow, dang, what is wrong with me? I didn't even recognize my own son. I lowered my head and kicked the gravel stones while I walked back to the pickup to get Linda. We met Aaron at the apartment, delivered the cat's paw, ate some cookies, and had a pleasant visit. And that's the first time I remember meeting Michelle. What a knockout. He sure made a good catch. Aaron's roommate, Doug, was also there with his visiting girlfriend.

From time to time, my wife Linda and I get a chuckle while we watch TV. I have to ask about the characters because they look so similar that I can't tell them apart. It gets confusing. Sometimes I get lost in the storyline.

An interesting side note, my mother thinks I look like Kevin Costner. I have verified with many trusted friends and relatives that I do not.

College of Southern Idaho (CSI), event.

I don't remember the event's name, but I remember I had planned on going for some time. I was excited the day had finally come. I decided to go alone. I left my home in Wendell and drove to Twin Falls at sunset. I was not very familiar with the campus. This was only the second or third time at CSI.

My sense of direction is not good. It has been compromised ever since the few years I lived in California. I'll explain. I was born in Massachusetts and lived there until I was 20. Whenever I traveled north, the ocean was on my right. Hence, I knew north was straight ahead. When I lived in southern Ca. the Pacific was on my right when traveling south. Get the picture? Now that I live in Idaho, there is no ocean. I look to the mountains as my guide. The Sawtooths are north. But when I go to Burley, there is no Sawtooth. It's the South Hills, but they are not in the north?

Nonetheless, the sun always rises in the east and sets in the west. But the sun had nearly set when I arrived at CSI. I drove around the large circular campus parking lots until I finally found an empty space.

Although the three-hour event was all I expected, I can't remember. It must be my old age. I do remember one thing about that night; it is unforget-table. There are some things a person would rather forget. But, anyway, the event concluded, and I was headed out of the auditorium. I couldn't remem-ber which door I had come in. I made a guess and picked one, door number two. I stepped outside and followed the sidewalk into the well-lit parking lot. Hmm, nothing looked familiar, wrong door. I started strolling through the aisles and rows of parked vehicles looking for my Blue S10 pickup. I came up empty in lot A. I came up empty in lot B. By this time, the parking lots were half empty. I continued my search through lot C. I stood there bewildered. Did someone steal my pickup? Exasperated, I began to walk back to lot A. Thirty minutes later, there were only a handful of vehicles left. Scratching my head, where is my pickup? Then I looked over by the corner pole light. Nearby in the shadow, something familiar. "Oh. Oh, yes, I remember." I didn't drive my truck to CSI. I took my wife's red Buick Skylark.

This is almost as embarrassing as when mom got in the wrong car when leaving Bob's Lobster. Two cars that look alike can be tricky. Word on the street says that eventually, you become your parents, hmm.

HOME

Amesbury, Massachusetts, home, or is it?

Memories of baseball in the overgrown, partially wooded meadow. My first speeding ticket. The day I drove the loud hand-painted big black 53 Oldsmobile down Highland Street, in the wealthy part of town. The speed limit was 25 MPH. My speedometer read 30. There he was, "puss gut." That's what we called the fat-bellied cop. I could see the gut protruding out from behind the elm tree.

I said, "Oh shit," as he stepped out from behind the tree, blew his whistle, and waved me over. He wrote me up.

Then there was the time Bob and I caught and grew worms to raise money for summer camping at Tuxbury Pond Campground.

Bob was a junior, and I a sophomore in High School.

Clinton Street, that's where Bob and I built the flying saucer. We spent several weekends building the eight-foot-tall, twelve-foot-wide, three-legged tripod covered with burlap and aluminum foil. The amber, green and red rotating below was the final touch. Bob and I recruited some vetted cohorts to carry the UFO from the forest to the middle of the road for a Halloween prank. The cops, fire department, and newspaper photographers all showed up.

Oh yeah, then the time my sweater caught on fire while

Wayne and I were playing football in his yard. I forgot that the match heads from my DIY match gun were still in my pocket. Darn, I loved that blue sweater with the burlap front.

There are memories of the flats, the flooded meadow where we used to ice skate. I still have the scar where Cheryl Blake stepped on my hand with her figure skates.

And there was the day it rained really hard. The temperature dropped to zero, and the whole town froze. No school that day. A bunch of us strapped on our skates and traveled all over town. The best part was when we skated up the nine-hole of the golf course, stopped at the top, turned around, and flew to the bottom.

In my first year in high school, we practiced a fire drill. Our class stood on Main Street across from the high school. We started joking,

"Wouldn't it be funny if the school was on fire?"

"Oh, look, smoke, smoke coming out the windows."

The smoke increased rapidly, then kaboom. The chemistry lab blew up. I finished high school at the old, once-abandoned Haverhill high school ten miles from Amesbury.

Just one week after I graduated from Wentworth Institute of

Technology in Boston, at the age of 20, I married my first wife. We packed our belongings into the purple Volkswagen and onto the homemade roof rack. And headed to California.

California, home, or is it?

We lived with the in-laws for a while until I found a job.

The only job I could find was in door-to-door sales. The ad read, "Work 4 hours a day, 4 days a week, $4 an hour". That was strange, not only the ad but also taking the job. I was afraid of people. I took an F in an English class in high school because I refused to do an impromptu talk on stage.

California was home for only three years. I was blessed with my first-born, a daughter, April, in Rialto.

Our neighbor, John H., who lived across the street from the in-laws, had a lovely house with a fabulous in-ground swimming pool. John was a risky individual. Once, he treated us to an all-expense-paid trip to Las Vegas. John maxed out all his credit cards. Debtors and the IRS were after him. He marked deceased on his mail and stuck it back in the mailbox. We took over the payments on his house, and he "vanished." This was our first house. I received a job promotion a year later and moved to El Cajon, California. We bought a house there. While we lived in El Cajon, I was blessed with a son, Aaron. Life got a little rough for us in California. My wife injured her back, Aaron was hospitalized with pneumonia, and my sales crew fell apart. We decided to move back to Massachusetts. But the most joyous and wonder-ful thing I remember about El Cajon was when I found Jesus and became born again.

We sold our house in El Cajon and paid off our debts. Dad flew to El Cajon and helped me drive the rental truck back to Amesbury. The wife and two kids traveled back by airplane.

We lived in Amesbury, Massachusetts, for three years. While in Massa-chusetts, my daughter Lori was born in Exeter, N.H. I worked two different dead-end jobs. When Lori was three months old, in 1977, my mother-in-law asked us to move to Idaho. They had had enough of that California life. Things got terrible in their neighborhood. I asked my mother-in-law, "Are there any trees there?" The first time we crossed through Idaho to visit a relative at Mountain Home Air Force Base, I commented, "Man, this is the nation's armpit. Who would ever want to live here"? But anyway, this is where we ended up, Wendell, Idaho, the "Hub City." I say, "It's nothing in the middle of everything."

Our move to Idaho was quite a journey. We couldn't afford a U-Haul truck, so we bought an old 66 GMC delivery van for $900. We purchased the fourteen-foot red and white box truck from a man and Wife who purchased the not-so-young vehicle in Florida for their move to Massachusetts. My brother-in-law, John, flew from Idaho to Massachusetts to drive our little blue Datsun with the wife and three kids to Idaho while I drove the "moving van" with April's cat. The brakes failed when the truck was loaded up and ready to go. We didn't even get out of the driveway. Dad and I fixed the brakes with the master cylinder ordered from Frazier's garage next door. The following day we headed out to Idaho. Ugh, the day we got to Idaho, the brakes went out again. Thankfully that happened as we parked the truck in the in-law's driveway in Filer. Later we sold the utility beast of burden to some friends, Steve and Anne, who were relocating to Texas. When they got to Colorado, the engine blew out. They replaced the tired old motor and continued to Texas. In Texas, somebody else bought the truck to move. If only trucks could tell stories?

We arrived here in Idaho in 1977. This is home now, or is it?

My second son, Luke, was born in Twin Falls, Idaho.

It was tough to adjust to the environment here in southern Idaho. It's immensely different than New England. I was used to everything being green, with lots of streams, rivers, lakes, ponds, and colorful autumn leaves. I miss the crashing Atlantic waves and the fragrant salty ocean air. But I've grown to love the shades of brown and hints of green here in southern Idaho. Oh, and the odor of dairies. One thing I enjoy is the friendly people. Another is the Idaho wave; hold onto the steering wheel and raise one or two fingers.

I've been here for forty-two years now. There are so many stories to tell. Stories of places, adventures, and people. Wendell is my home, or is it? No, it's not my home. There has been another place prepared for me. I'm waiting for that glorious day!

THE CRAWDAD HOLE AND AN AMERICAN INDIAN RECIPE

The wobbly dude didn't have a sack on his back, but a large, smelly bucket hung from his left hand. His clothing was ragged and his gray hair, what was left of it, was dirty and unkempt. He greeted us with a partially toothless smile that showed past his brown-skinned face.

"Howdy." He imparted spittle when he spoke....

I had never seen this guy before today. But this is how our day of the visit to Malad Gorge was interrupted. One of my favorite places is the gorge. Not the main gorge but the "secret" little horseshoe canyon tucked away off the beaten path parallel to the Malad Gorge State Park.

Many years ago, one of my native Idaho friends introduced me to this incredible place, to crawdads and the art of crawdad fishing. Crawdads are freshwater crustaceans. Tiny lobsters. They are usually 4 inches to 6 inches for good size ones. I take the kids there for this fun adventure.

This is how our day went:

"Hey, boys, do you want to go crawdad fishing today?"

Aaron and Luke excitedly responded, "Yeah, what time, dad?"

"As soon as we can get ready," I answered, "We need to gather the stuff. We need a bucket, a small net, string, and some bacon."

Luke asked, "Bacon?"

"Yep, bacon for bait," I said with a chuckle.

After we gathered the fishing stuff, we drove to Hagerman. There is only one way you get to the fishing spot unless you want to climb down a 200-foot canyon wall. We turned off Hwy.30 just before the bridge at the

Malad River. We drove up the gravel washboard road about a half-mile to the locked gate. There is a small space between the iron poles to pass right beside the "No Trespassing" sign. It's at least a mile hike to the dam on the hilly gravel road. The lava rock canyon walls tower above the right-hand side of the road. One hundred feet below the left side of the road, the Malad River roars fiercely as the water crashes over the rocks. It's so loud that it drowns out our conversation as we take the tiring journey. (Sometimes, we would stop at a shady spot and grab a bite from a makeshift lunch. And do a rock-throwing contest to see who can reach the other side of the canyon over the river.) Eventually, we arrive at the gate by the dam and pass by another "No trespassing" and "Danger" sign. The gravel road ends at some steps on the south side of the dam. We crossed over the top of the dam, then turned a sharp left and dropped down about 10 feet. Then followed the gnarly path alongside the tall 15-foot concrete diversion coulee wall. This path winds for about 50 yards before reaching the canyon opening of the crystal clear spring-fed stream. The stream is filled with huge boulders, some taller than a 10-year-old.

We encountered the strange man on our way into the rock climbing area. He stood partially blocking the path with his smelly bucket

"Howdy." He spittled a little as he spoke.

"Hi." I guarded the boys, "Nice day."

The gentle breeze carried the odor of fish and bourbon,

"Yep." He groaned. "Got me some crawdads. See you got equipment, goin fishin?"

I smiled, "Yep, we're going to catch some crawdads. What are you going to do with all your crawdads?"

"Well, I'm goin to eat 'em. What else ya supposed to do with 'em?"

I shrugged a shoulder, "Throw them back in. It's just fun to catch them. Hmm, how do you cook and eat them?"

He chuckled and sucked back a little drool from his bottom lip. He stuck his hand in the bucket and pulled out a live crawdad a little longer than his fingers.

"Cook 'em?" He replied. "I eat 'em like the Indians use to eat 'em, like the owls. You know how owls eat?"

"Yeah," I replied. Aaron and Luke stood beside me, watching-waiting.

Without hesitation, he responded in his moist, slurry speech. "The owl eats live food, then pukes the leftovers in a pellet. Like this-ya know. It's the Indian recipe." He opened his mouth wide, showing his few yellow crooked teeth, and chomped down on the crawdad. Then took another bite until the whole thing was in his mouth and began chewing. Chewing and rolling the pieces in his mouth. Crunching and slobbering, inwardly gathering the indigestible parts into a clump. He spits the bony chunk onto the ground. Then he pulls one out of the bucket and extends the wiggly morsel towards us as he says,

"There, that's how ya eat 'em. Wana try one?"

"No, thank you." I excused myself and the boys as we slithered by the drunken pioneer.

We headed up the boulder-filled canyon, climbing over and around the smooth jumbo rocks and between the small pools of crystal clear water looking for an ideal place to fish. We found a good spot, tied a piece of bacon on the line, and carefully lowered it into the pool near some rock crevasses. After a short time, the little critters crawled out from under the rocks and started latching onto the bacon. One by one. We skillfully pulled up three or four at a time as they clung to the bacon.

"We got some, dad, we got some." They proclaimed in unison.

"Bravo, boys, bravo."

We did try cooking and eating some crawdads once. We boiled salted water and dumped them in, like cooking a lobster. I think they are gross. I'll just keep throwing them back. The hiking, climbing, picnicking, and fishing makes for an enjoyable family afternoon. My grandchildren sometimes go to this "secret" magical spot. Maybe even my great-grandchildren will go someday. Love Idaho.

There is an old-time song called "Crawdad Song." The ballad evolved from Anglo-American play-party traditions and African-American blues. Workers building levees to prevent the flooding of the Mississippi River in the south may have been among the first to sing it. It would be a fun song (the kid's version) to learn to sing quietly while fishing or hiking on the way to the crawdad hole. Even a Yankee guy like me can learn a fine southern song.

"You get a line, and I'll get a pole, honey.
You get a line, and I'll get a pole, babe.
You get a line, and I'll get a pole
We'll go fishin' in the crawdad hole

CHAIN SAW

The "Earth Stove" there it is in the corner. The black, four-legged wood burner. I had never lived in a house with one of these things before. Back when I was in high school, the Smiths had one. Their winter home was always so warm. The aroma of burning pine and a slight haze of smoke in their home made it seem so laid back. Their clothes even have that woody scent they carry with them where ever they go. But that was 54 years ago, back in 1965.

So here I am in our newly bought baby poop brown home, a 1976 FHA bread box cookie-cutter house with torn-up vinyl floors, dark wood panel accent wall, and low boy toilets.

I told Linda, "Well, if we have a wood-burning stove, I better get some wood. I better get me a chainsaw."

I've seen them on T.V., in stores, in magazines, and in picture books. But I never held one or touched one. They look rather scary. What the heck? I can do it. I found one in the "Harbor Freight" catalog. Their banner reads,

"Quality tools at ridiculously low prices." I've bought stuff at their store before, "quality" is a pretty subjective opinion. But anyway, it would be a cheap way to get started with this timber-cutting adventure. The printed "super coupon" Ad stated, "Poulan rebuilt 14" gas chain saw, $49." I picked up the phone and ordered the saw. Several days later, the UPS guy delivered the short green grizzly tooth gas-powered mini monster. It came with an owner's instruction and safety manual. The information on how to start the saw and maintain it was helpful; put in the bar oil, mix the fuel, pour in the fuel, prime it 10x, pull out the choke, pull the cord 5x, push the choke in halfway, pull the cord. There you have it-one loud potential flesh-gorging and delimbing tool for $49.

Chain saw safety; here is a quote from Carl Smith (no relation to the Smiths as mentioned earlier), "If you place your hands on a chain saw, you must keep in mind that it is like grabbing a hand grenade without a pin in it. It is very likely to go off in your face. From the moment that you… The chainsaw is the most dangerous hand tool that can be purchased on the open market. It requires no training to own or operate. An overall average of 40,000 injuries and deaths occur annually… ". *It's not in my DNA, but I'll figure it out.*

I headed to the Forest Service Office and bought my South Hills wood-cutting permit.

My oldest son, Aaron, and I went to the South Hills. We borrowed my brother-in-law's pickup truck to pull our 16' Wells Cargo enclosed trailer to the South Hills. We filled the box trailer with 8' and 4' logs. We almost got Bruce's truck stuck between some trees and spent half the day wrestling one of those lodge pole pines out of the tangle in the treetops.

Another time Chad and I went up by Alturas Lake. It was mid-October. I borrowed my friend Blaine's pickup bed trailer, a ratty-looking blue ¾ ton. We found a small grove of dead-standing lodge pole pines on the other side of a little snow-covered meadow. I backed the trailer up with my two-wheel-drive Chevy Blazer and started cutting. I felled a couple of the slender, nearly limbless pines. When I was ready to yell another "timber" to drop the big one. I turned around to see where Chad, my 12-year-old, was.

But he was nowhere to be seen. I looked over the knoll behind me. There he was, wading out of a shin-deep frozen pool of water. He discovered that the ice was too thin to hold him. We loaded the cut wood and tried to drive out of the meadow but to no avail. My tires just kept spinning. After we managed to get out of the field, we pulled off the side of the road just a few yards away to cut some more trees. We were really getting into it.

"Dad, look, someone's coming."

I replied, "It's a Ranger."

With a furrowed brow, he stepped out of his truck and checked to ensure I had the proper permit and equipment. And to confirm, I would tag my load before I moved my vehicle. He scanned the torn-up meadow behind the "No vehicle beyond this point" sign.

Then he asked, "Did you cut this trailer of wood from the spot where you are at?"

I lied, "Yes, off this little hill." We knew he knew. Got away with that one. But my conscience still bothers me.

One year the grandkids came with us. We camped for the week, got all our woodcut, and loaded on the first day.

Every year it's a new family story. Getting snowed on, flat tires, trees hung up in other trees, campfires, mom worried about wandering kids getting lost.

I look forward to yearly wood cutting and feeling the warmth of the wood-burning stove, the smoky aroma, and the family time together. So far, no grave personal injuries. I'll continue as long as they want to keep cutting wood. Hopefully, the grandkids will get a wood-burning stove someday.

I never dreamt how a little potential, flesh-gorging, delimbing device could bring the family together... for good times. A worthy tool for bonding-sweat equity. Ahh, the irony, the saw that cuts is what bonds the family together.

IT'S NOT HADDOCK

Mom doesn't avoid saying what's on her mind. It's pretty comical at times.

Noon was fast approaching; mom and I sat at her kitchen table. Bob's Lobster was closed on Tuesdays, her favorite place to eat. We always go to Bob's at least once during my 10-day annual visit. For some reason, neither her friends nor relatives ever want to take her there. But she loves that fresh fish, especially the Haddock. No one can cook how Bob's Lobster prepares daily caught Haddock and varieties of Atlantic fish and crustaceans. She and dad used to go there frequently. Dad passed away 6 years ago. Due to her last illness, she has not recovered thoroughly enough to drive (everyone is glad she doesn't drive anymore). We had already gone there once since I arrived last Thursday. So we decided to go to The Hungry Hunter for lunch this time.

We arrived at The Hungry Hunter at about 1 o'clock. The hostess greeted us, ushered us to our seats, and then returned with the information board, a two-foot-wide by a three-foot-tall whiteboard with large black letters, easy for mom to read. She presented us with the regular menu. I ordered Shepard's pie. Mom was having difficulty deciding what to order.

She questioned me," Do you think the Haddock is a good choice?"

"You should choose something else, mom, because you always complain about the Haddock where ever you eat, except at Bob's Lobster."

But she ordered the Haddock anyway to test whether it would be good. The server brought out the meals. Mom took a bite of the Haddock and thought the first bite was ok, especially the breaded coating. After the third bite, she was not so sure.

Then proclaimed to me, "This is not Haddock."

She was sure of it, as confident as a chicken is not a fish.

She said, "This restaurant, like all the others, claims it is Haddock, but it is really Cod or Scrod."

We finished our meal through grumbling and complaining.

My Shepard's pie was delicious. We boxed up our leftovers and walked toward the exit.

The hostess was very polite, escorting us to the door when she asked, "How was everything?"

Mom blurted out, "It wasn't Haddock."

The hostess responded, "I'm sorry. What do you mean?"

Mom said, "It wasn't Haddock!"

"What do you mean it wasn't Haddock?"

"Just what I said. It wasn't Haddock. They might tell you it's Haddock, but I know what Haddock tastes like, and that isn't Haddock."

"I'm sorry, mam, but it is Haddock. I saw the cook take it out of the refrigerator, cut up the fish, and put it on the grill. It's Haddock!"

Mom stared at the hostess, "It isn't Haddock."

From behind mom, I smirked at the hostess. *If I tell the hostess she's not winning this argument, she may take my comment wrong.*

I held my tongue and nodded.

I helped mom across the parking lot and into the car. Before shutting the door, I asked, "Mom, Do you want me to go back inside and go into the kitchen and look at the fish?"

While we were eating our meal, mom complained. So I googled "Haddock" and saw pictures and got information about the texture and flavor of Haddock compared to other close varieties like cod and scrod.

After a thoughtful pause, she commented, "No, I know it's not Haddock. You don't need to check. I just read an article in the newspaper about a survey taken at the area restaurants and the restaurants' false claims about serving Haddock."

Being around mom is not dull. Older is bolder. We laugh together when we talk about the fishy restaurant experience.

It's good to do things she wants while still with us. At age 88, I don't know how many years she has left. I enjoy her company.

A MAN CALLED WILLIE

The rugged young lad, Willie, was embarrassed. All his friends had single-runner hockey skates. He begged his parents for skates to shoot the puck on the stiff water of the New England pond. The day came when his folks came through with his request. However, for whatever reason, the skates were not single runners but double runners. He suffered through the humiliation until he could buy his own single runners.

The young Willie powered through his paper route to earn his own money. The spring was wet, the summer was hot, the fall crisp, and the winter icy. Paydays came. Instead of buying the things he wanted, his WWI veteran father and mother made him use his money to buy clothes. His parents had survived the great depression, lost their Taylor shop business, and endured many other hardships.

At age 18, the particular letter came, greetings from Uncle Sam, "report to the U.S. Army recruiting office." He was trained and assigned to the armored division. Maybe the army appointed him to the tank division because his pant leg size is only 26 inches. Fortunately, while on the ship to Okinawa, the enemy surrendered.

Though he was small, he did not have a "Napoleon complex"; he did not need a big truck, was not overly aggressive, or spoke in a loud voice. He could dribble the ball and shoot the hoop as well as anyone, moved like a cat.

He married two years after his discharge from the army. He is the father of two sons and a daughter. My dad, Willie, worked at least two jobs, sometimes as many as four. He always fed his family and took proper care of his possessions.

We spent most of our time together, working. One summer, when I was twelve, I helped dad paint Mr. Hill's 3 story stately home. The historic captain's home was located in Newburyport. He put the heavy forty-foot wood extension ladder on top of the toolbox in the back of his pickup truck. He cantilevered the ladder off the edge of the lower-story porch roof. While the top teetered in mid-air so he could reach the 3rd story fascia (wood trim at the roof's edge). I sat on the bottom of the ladder to "stabilize" it. He used a four-inch-wide paintbrush out of a gallon can, so he was up there for a long time.

He painted in the evenings, after his regular job, and on weekends. That big old mansion took a whole summer to paint.

Dad was a gorilla. One time I remember it took three adults to hold him down while mom put eye drops in his eyes.

He had robust attitudes and views. His neighbor and friend, Chip, had a dog that would shit in our yard. Dad told him to keep control of the mutt. Well, that didn't happen. Dad would gather up the crap and give it back to Chip or put it on Chip's porch. The feud continued for some time. Things finally got worked out; the fecal matter quit coming.

They remained good friends. When Chip worked nights, Dad would snow blow Chip's driveway. Dad would sometimes mow Chip's lawn. Chip returns the favor now that dad is gone; Leukemia got him. Chip mows mom's lawn and plows her driveway. Dad passed away on June 27, 2011, at age 84.

There was a certain sadness behind his kind smile. "Cheated, it's not fair," he would say. The monster slew dad in just three months. The dream of lengthy retirement vanished.

My absence brought him sorrow, but our visits brought us joy. My tears remind me that there is not enough time. Seasons come and go, but there is a finality to it all.

SIX

MOVING FORWARD

FADED MEMORIES

I sit at the kitchen table, meditating. Staring at the snapshot. Jim Irons and Shane Brown, creative writing class instructors at the College of Southern Idaho (CSI), assigned us to write a non-fiction story from a photograph. So I pluck at the keyboard's keys while pondering this photo.

Two plastic tubs sitting on their Grandma's wooden porch, each filled with water in the sweltering June sun. A boy and a girl each, with a gun. The naked Cheshire boy splashes with a grin. His sister smiling, pointed pistol in hand. Nearly submerged, cooling herself from the scorching sun.

The memory is hidden in a sunken-locked pirate chest. Deep in the recesses of my mind, I cannot find the memory even with the photograph - my daughter, my son, no memory of it at all. They are having fun. Brother and sister with two squirt guns.

My chest pounding with anxiety. My eyes are waterfalls. The memory is in the back of my brain, sealed away, out of sight. It's not my fault, I know. But I'm in agony. My little ones are now so tall. They're grown and have children of their own. If only a photograph could heal an old man's recall. How much more can I not remember?

SLOWING DOWN

Musings and a Prayer

He was eighty-three. He got leukemia and died at age eighty-four. He wanted to slow down, to retire.

I could get a steady part-time job and buy my second car at sixteen. $100 cash for the twelve-year-old hand-painted, loud, beautiful black Oldsmobile. I sold my newer red and white tail-finned '57 Plymouth Fury for $30. That's what I paid for it the year before. I used the $30 toward the '53 Oldsmobile.

One day I left Howie's house in the black beauty, destined for home. I turned off Route 110 and headed down Hillside Avenue. I stomped on the gas, listened to the engine roar, and rolled by the ancient elm trees lining each side of the street. The elegant two-story Victorian homes had well-groomed yards. The gas gauge sped toward E, and the speedometer crept up; fifteen, sixteen, seventeen, twenty miles per hour. The engine continued to roar for a quarter-mile. Officer Antell, AKA "puss-gut," named by the local teens, popped out from behind an Elm. He stood in his bright blue uniform, bulging at the belly, with his right hand on the bill of his fancy blue cap. Then he blew his whistle and signaled me to pull over. I slowed down and stopped at the curb.

He asked me. "Where are you going in such a hurry?"

"Home," I replied. "I'm headed home."

I received my first speeding ticket. Thirty-five miles per hour in a twenty-five-mile-per-hour zone.

Ten years later, I was driving on the San Diego I-15 in my new hot luxury Pontiac Grand Prix. I looked in my rearview mirror and saw the Bear's red and blue flashing lights. I slowed down and moved into the breakdown lane. The trooper strolled up to the Pontiac, poised himself at the driver's door, and motioned me to roll down my window.

"Do you know how fast you were going?" he asked.

I replied like a boy caught with his hand in the cookie jar. "I'm not sure, officer, maybe sixty-five?"

He looked at me with a stern straight face and said, "I clocked you at seventy-six miles per hour. The speed limit is fifty-five."

I slumped down in my seat with puppy-dog eyes. I responded, "But, officer, I was going downhill."

I received my second speeding ticket.

At age sixty-two, I drove slower, most of the time. Now that I get social security, many things are slower; getting off the couch, chewing food, doing math, going pee…. If slowing down means sitting on the couch, I can't do it.

Dad fully retired when he was eighty-two. After retirement, he got leukemia. It came on suddenly. The oncologist told him he had three to six months. It hit him hard. He died three weeks before his eighty-fifth birthday.

When he quit his greeter job at Sam's Club (a membership-only retail warehouse owned by Walmart Inc.), he looked forward to a peaceful retirement. In his last few months, he rode in the electric shopping cart at Sam's and visited his friends.

"It's not fair," he would say. I watched him dry a tear each time he shared his thoughts about his demise. He was robbed of his retirement life. Our whole family was robbed.

Sam's Club had an annual review/evaluation of its employees. They would give out pay raises to those who qualified. At dad's evaluation, they told him that he would have to smile when he greeted customers to earn his five-cent raise.

Dad's reply, as mom told me, "I'm not going to smile."

He didn't get the raise. However, they did give him a nice large wood plaque for his many years of service at his retirement.

I'm seventy-one, retired, and getting old. It's like being a can of Campbell's Chunky Pub-Style Chicken Pot Pie Soup. Yeah, canned soup. Before the canning, all the peas, carrots, potatoes, and chicken had life. They were growing. They had a purpose. A destiny. Look at them now. They are all sequestered, chunky, and embalmed in chemicals. Nowhere to go, nothing to do. They just rest there. Waiting. Being retired is like that. I'm trying to figure it out, slowing down, hmmm. But hold on. Patience is crucial. My expiration date is not legible. I'm looking for the can opener.

Lord, open my lid, pour me out into the pan. Put me on the stove, heat me up, and stir me occasionally. Help me to be the can's back label message; 'Be Bold, Be You. Embrace Hearty.'

FIGHTING BACK FOR PASSION

-Dear God-

When Bob Ignot introduced himself, I was very uncomfortable. At a dark hour, he knocked on our door at the request of Cousins Steve and Teresa. He tried to explain the sundering breach, but I could not make sense of it, or should I say I didn't understand. Later that night, a glimmer of light pierced through the fog in my head, so I inquired for more information. Bob further explained Your heart. You appeared to be willful with the resources to fix things. Later I told Bob that I wanted to know more. He invited me to meet with some of Your friends, Steve Lembke, Teresa (Steve's wife), John, and a young lady, Zoey.

Bob said his Pastor, Tom Faye, would not be there, but that was OK because the group often met without him. Tom was a busy man. I didn't meet Tom until a few weeks later. We all met Wednesday evening and nearly every week after that, as You remember. It was about the third week I fell in love with You. Every morning, I would eagerly wake up looking forward to our day together. The more I got to know You, the more committed I became. It was like a burning ember igniting a bonfire. I spoke of You to almost everyone.

One particular day at the El Cajon city park, Tom and several of Your friends and I met at the swimming pool. I got dunked, submerged, and baptized that day. Things changed between us. At least for me. My love for You burst into flames when I emerged from the water. I know You felt it too. So I don't have to explain that to You. You know what I'm talking about.

But what came next was not pleasant. When I introduced You to people I didn't know, strangers, or even friends and relatives, they were offended or angry. Some squirmed.

It became nearly impossible to live in El Cajon. My conscience was convicted of some unethical work practices. I quit my sales career resulting in unbearable financial hardship. I listened to You and took Your leading. I totally trusted You, Jesus.

Sometimes I still don't understand why You want me to do certain things.

It was difficult to leave our California friends and move back to Massachusetts. However, shortly after arriving at Amesbury, You introduced me to some of Your east coast ambassadors. First, there was the teacher preacher, John, and then Don. Don was a soft-spoken bookstore owner of salty material located in the neighboring maritime city of Newburyport. His eyes smiled when he spoke. Dining with Don made me thirsty, thirsty for You. Remember those days?

When I visited Don, he introduced me to Kirk, a compassionate retired Naval Officer. So many people know You. I loved what You wrote and revealed to Kirk. He shared Your wisdom with me; I put much to memory. Stored away for necessary times. Moments when I needed boldness, encouragement, comfort, discernment, hope, wisdom....

You and I were co-workers in Amesbury. I don't have to remind You of the closeness we shared there. Remember the bus people? They came in from Chicago. They were crazy for You, Jesus, all excited, celebrating endlessly. They were contagious. Fantastic, every one of them. We had some good times with them together, You and I.

During their visit, they made many friends. When they left town, some of the townspeople went with them. Alan, my friend Bill's brother, joined them on the bus. But not everyone was happy with the Jesus bus people. Alan's parents, Gene and Pauline, were furious. "He joined a cult." They said.

Some people were deeply grieved, and families became divided. Some townsfolk were confused and unsettled about Your Gospel. We visited some of those stressed people. Remember? People are so stubborn they do not want your help. What I experienced with You inspired me to love You even more. If that were possible. There is more I could pen about us in Amesbury, but I do not have time to write it all.

A couple of years later, I moved from Massachusetts to southern Idaho. I was stuck in Amesbury. I sensed from You that I was at a dead-end - my job, my future, nothing moved forward—time to go. So I did. At first, Idaho was a dry place, not only the desert, sagebrush, and lava rock but also the friendly people. I searched for Your friends and found some in Wendell. I enjoyed being with them for a short period. I became warm to Tim and Dave. Steve and Ann Bennett became close friends as well. Soon after that, I met Jeff and Becky.

Remember when You pushed me to dog Steve Gilbert through Simerly's market? I cornered him as his wife Cathy smirked in the background, pleased that someone finally confronted him. I threw Steve a bone. Soon afterward,

Steve, his wife Cathy, Cathy's twin sister Deanna, her husband Pete, and I began hanging out. Remember when I introduced You to Steve? You made a difference in him, from rebellious and dead to a new life. Working with You ushered the hound out of me.

But after a while, trouble was on the doorstep. Tim, Dave, and I approached a few of Your followers about their waywardness. They did not accept our concerns. I distanced myself from them because of my love for You.

As I grew to know You more intimately, I realized people either embraced Your friendship or became disturbed. There is a sea of ashes, unsettledness, anger, or unspoken harbors of resentment in those of hardened soil. I know Your heart and the sadness all this brings to You.

You guided me to more of Your believers in Jerome. You have so many adopted children. I was not emotionally and spiritually broken but in need of like-mindedness. You guided me to Randy, Dianne, Dave, Wendy, Richard, and Deane. Oh, remember how many times we enjoyed our lives together? How hard we worked with You. How we grew closer to each other. There were some tough times, especially for me. Personal things. Even though I love You, I became angry at You. I blamed You for my marriage break-up. I distanced myself from You. For a while, perhaps for too long.

Tears were my companion for weeks. Tears of loss. Loss of a marriage, then the loss of You. I shut You out, remember? I came to my senses when I realized You were not going anywhere. It was me that had gone away. I know You are compassionate and forgiving. I'm fighting back. Sometimes with tears. It's been years. I need You to do it; I can't recover through my human strength.

After several months of divorced loneliness, I pleaded with You. Provide me a soul mate who loves You as much as I do. You came through. Why should I doubt You? A precious gift you gave me. Linda and I married four months after coming together. We have had almost twenty-eight years with You. What a blessing.

Trouble again, this time in Jerome. The human desire for power and control severed relationships. I'm sorry for my weakness. But I can't go back. I trust in You but not the institution. Has this strained our relationship?

Sometimes I feel we have restored that passionate union. But often, the emptiness overwhelms me. How do I fight back to regain my passion for You? My eyes are moist with hope. What is wrong with me? I struggle to regain what I lost with You. My attitude, my language, and my actions, most of which are unattractive of what You want. The vessel that once held the fullness of passion perfume is nearly empty. But I know, Lord, that You will overflow my cup again. You are my hope, and I trust in You.

WHACKED, JUMPED, AND ON THE EDGE

Whacked.

1995, Wendell, Idaho. A sharp smack on the back of my head came out of nowhere, "Damn, that hurt." I dropped the long piece of corrugated roofing metal. I caught my balance and turned around to see what was behind me. Zilch. I turned back around and picked up the tin roofing. I tried again to wedge the metal between the tall, stout wood pole and under the existing roof metal to complete the repair of the loafing shed. Wham, "Damn," my head got another blow. I threw down the galvanized metal and spun around to see what whacked my head.

I looked at Aaron, "Did you see what hit me?"

He replied, "Didn't see anything, dad. What are you yakking about? Come on, let's get this done."

"No," I replied, "When I bend over and slide the metal underneath, I get thumped in the back of the head."

"Nothing over here, dad. Your nuts," He replied. "Come on, let's get this done."

I countered, "Well, I'm not doing it again. Twice is enough."

I gathered my wits about me. *I'll figure this out.* I spotted a bare wire in front of me stapled to the shed side of the pole.

I proclaimed, "Oh crap, that's an electric fence wire. I get it."

"Ha, sounds good, dad. Come on, let's get this done."

Jumped

1991, Gooding Idaho. I gutted the musty old kitchen; tore out this small cape-style house's cabinets, flooring, and drywall. I threw all the debris out the back door and made a massive pile of broken, jagged, and nail-riddled boards.

Today is the day to install the range exhaust fan onto the roof. I tore off some of the old green mossy wood shingles. Wielding my Diablo Steel Demon-toothed long-bladed Makita Sawzall, I cut a hole in the roof boards. The sun became more obscure as the clouds increased. There's a little rumble off in the distance. The clouds turned black, and the breeze blew a little stronger. Whew, I'm almost done. I installed the galvanized metal flashing around the range vent exhaust hood. *Six more nails to pound, and I'll be done.* There is a slight drizzle, but I can finish before the rain. *That's it, the last nail.* I caught sight of a little old chubby lady walking through the alley behind the house. She gazed up at me as I prepared to climb off the roof. I stood up. *Whoa.* I employed the downhill skiing abilities that I reaped from Soldier Mountain. The roof slope was between a Black Diamond and Blue Square. From the ally came a shriek.

"Oh my God, are you alright?"

She observed my skillful descent down the roof and the dramatic leap from the roof's edge to miss the pile of wreckage below. When my feet hit the ground, I performed my brown belt self-defense Aikido skill of the forward roll.

"Yes, mam, I'm fine, thank you."

On the edge

1980, Jerome, Idaho. I've worked for Larry, the farmer turned building contractor, for two years. He is an accomplished, forward, thinking guy. He puts my construction science degree to practical, hands-on use. We make a great team. He's tall and right-handed. I'm short and left-handed. The home building industry in Idaho is beginning to catch up with more modern construction concepts, like roof trusses, instead of hand-framed rafters. 4'x 8' plywood instead of 1" x 12" boards. Also, the use of pneumatic tools, like framing and roofing nailers. Air tools sure beat pounding tons of nails by hand.

Today we installed the ridge shingles on Britton's two-story house.

Larry said, "Hey, Glenn, I need you to put on the ridge cap with the new coil nailer. Can you handle that? I'm headed to town for supplies."

"Yep," I replied, "Got it."

He squeezed his tall, lanky body into the front seat of his compact yellow Datsun King Cab pick-up. His tailgate disappeared beyond the sagebrush.

I fired up the air compressor, drug out the air hose, and got all set up.

I climbed up the ladder. The racket of the air compressor sounded below. With the gun in hand. Bam, bam, bam. Bent over, walking backward. Putting down and nailing one shingle after another, dragging the red rubber hose. Bam, bam. Bam, bam. Awesome.

Whoa! I find myself at the edge of the roof. My back to the air. My feet' balls rested on the roof's outer edge. Ahead of me is the whole roof. Behind me, nothing. I grab the "red rubber lifeline" with both hands and pull. Hand over hand. Rapidly. I get nothing but hose. My body starts tilting backward, little by little. I begin preparing my mind for the fall. There is nothing but hose in front of me, lots of hose.

What happens next is hard to explain. There is pressure on my back. My body begins to go from slanted to upright. I can't believe I'm standing straight up, complete balance. I step onto the roof, my head tilts upward, and I sigh. *In the "Good Book," I once read in my maker's instruction manual, "The angel of the Lord encamps around those who fear Him and rescues them." Hmm?* Time to turn around and finish nailing the job. Bam, Bam. Bam, bam, bam. Job complete. I didn't say anything to Larry about the gravity of the encounter.

SNIPPETS

I flip through a few more pages and photos of happy, loving, and cheerful faces. Pictures of family, friends, our pastors, and employers. But there is one picture of a tall, thin man with amber lens glasses. He has a slight grin, scruffy chin, beard, and mustache. A friend.

March 1993. I walked down the Jerome courthouse steps. I shouted, "Wow, it's over, finally over. I'm free."

September 1993. It's finally come true. The woman of my prayers and dreams, my soul mate, Linda. Like me, a lover of the Lord Jesus.

2019, I look through the wedding photo album for memories. Unexpected tears begin to fill my eyes. I see pictures of my beautiful bride, family members, good friends, relatives, and fellow church members as I flip through the pages. Some mere acquaintances. Each one has a story.

Little did I know that divorce is never the end? Life goes on. More joyful times indeed are to be had. But a whack-a-mo life has begun. Cathy, the ex-wife, was not done with her craftiness and destructive toxic pattern.

Each picture in mine and Linda's wedding album, my dear sweet, and incredible wife, brings another memory. Another story, another life. Jogging my memory with tears of joy and heartache, with… hmm, I realize that after years of numbness, I can't identify most of my feelings. How did I come to this state? I sit here and get teary, but I don't know why.

Some photos:

On the first page, my bride stands with a wrinkle-free, beautiful smile, holding the wedding bouquet. Another photo of Ray and Marion, my future father-in-law and mother-in-law. Wisconsinites. Missing are my mom and dad, unable to make the trip from Massachusetts. Dad met Linda before the wedding on his memorable visit to Wendell. He bought us a set of pots and pans as a wedding gift. I sure miss Dad. He passed away on June 27, 2011.

Second page: my sixteen-year-old daughter, Lori, the bride's maid. Dressed in a forest green velvet sculpt off-the-shoulder dress. Beautiful and stunning. And her best friend Teri, maid of honor, dressed in the same manner. Tears begin to well up as memories of the independent, strong-willed diamond daughter come to mind. I sure miss my stubborn little one. She passed away on September 18, 2014, due to a stroke. That happened on Linda's and my 21st.anniversary.

My eldest daughter April, age 20, adjusting my tie. Her beautiful smile and glamorous pose. Then there is Aaron, my nineteen-year-old, Standing straight and strong. His Head held high, but his eyes and mouth tell a different story. Oh, my soon-to-be two other children, Karissa, age five, and Chad, one month shy of three. I love them dearly and am looking forward to being their new dad.

Third page: The vows. A beautiful bride with a glowing smile and love-fixed eyes. A full dark bearded groom with a crown of gray and a joyful spirit. He is fixed hard and fast, eye to eye with his bride. Then there's young Luke, my eleven-year-old with his usual gleaming smile. He was too reserved to share his thoughts and feelings. The peacemaker. Also, there is proud Pastor Randy, all suited up with his small bush mustache, reading the scripture and the duty of the wedding vows. And another photo of Aaron, head not so high and a somber look on his face. I was so caught up in the moment that his apparent discontent totally escaped me. And my dear friend Becky, Singing Linda's and my wedding song, "Our Love In Christ" by Kelly Willard. As I write this memory at this moment, I pause, hold Linda in my arms and begin a gentle sobbing.

Turn a few more pages and more photos: Johnny, my beloved 45- year-old friend and brother in the Lord. He has cerebral palsy. Smiling and all dressed up. He's a hero and an inspiration to many people. All the things he has overcome despite his challenges. He is always a heartwarming character and loves riding his trike and visiting the townspeople. I miss Johnny and his hugs. He has moved to northern Idaho. He reminds me of my brother, Ted, also handicapped, who passed away in 2002 at forty-nine. Ted lived far beyond his expected years due to the constant loving care of his mom. She cared for him his entire life at home, despite all the criticism of that culture to put Ted in an institution. I miss my little brother. He was not at our wedding.

There is a picture of Jessie, Jeanne, Bonnie, Roger, and others. We seldom, if ever, see these friends anymore. Then the image of mom and dad Smith, my new beautiful in-laws. I miss mom and dad Smith. They passed away in 2013, nine months apart from each other. A picture of my daughter April and her boyfriend Stan. Oh, Stan, there is some dark, dreadful story about Stan. April has never divulged the details to me. I have my guess, but I haven't had that conversation with her. Some things are better left not uncovered.

I flip through a few more pages and photos of happy, loving, and cheerful faces. Oh, the smiling faces, all the veiled layers behind the cheerfulness.

More pages: In the background, a picture of that man standing tall, with thin, amber-lens glasses. He has a slight grin, scruffy chin, beard, and mustache. A friend. Later I find out he is a strong suspect of having an affair with my ex. I'll never find out for sure. Some things are better not to uncover. But I know for sure she has had other men. Our children and I were abandoned. But God is good!

Next page: we are bride and groom, all casual now. Smiling and waving goodbye. We are driving the blue S15 Chevy pick-up truck that dad gave me to Jackson, Wyoming, for our honeymoon. We are leaving the turmoil of life behind for a while.

ON BEING A HOME INSPECTOR

I sat down; sawdust filled the air. *Breathe in, breathe out, breathe in, breathe out...* Burning to death or drowning are my two biggest fears of ways to die. I'm not afraid to die; I know my destiny. It is the pain, the suffering. Scorched or suffocated. I'd choose to not breathe, but not today.

The pulmonologist gave me the inhaler last week and instructed me to find a different occupation. My lungs' tiny air sacs (alveoli) were saturated with sawdust. The inevitable, shortened life if I continued my carpenter occupation.

I took the Doc's advice. Nine months later, I was on my way to my new vocation.

Home inspectors do not receive combat pay. Neither did Home inspector training provide me with armadillo skin. I need the armor to defend disgruntled vicious homeowners, rabid realtors, and sue-happy buyers. Or protection from the high expectancy, picky, you don't do that here, Californians? Also, the ability to battle with serpents, protective canines, skeletal remains and dead fury cats, animal shit, electrocution hazards, slippery roofs, and falling ladders...

The following is a sample of my fun life as the inspector.

I labeled my first inspection "aliens of the turd kind." After completing the inspection checklist in the main abandoned house, I crossed the patio to inspect the vacant mother-in-law's apartment. I opened the door. A stench of raw sewerage greeted me. The entire apartment floor was covered in ankle-deep human waste. I did not enter the lagoon. Welcome to the inspection industry.

Occasionally I traveled to Fairfield, a forty-six-mile journey. The house was remodeled by a hack. There was a long list of items that were not correctly done and many dangerous electrical issues. Oh yes, and the strange green lizard-looking creature with bulging eyes in the damp crawl space under the house.

I introduce the first rabid realtor to you, the seller's agent, Greg.

You son of a bitch, you killed the deal. You killed the deal. You'll never work in this area again, never."

At this point, I'm mentioning a disclaimer to protect the innocent. Many realtors look out for their clients; this guy was not one of them. Also, in the mid-'90s, home inspections were not very common.

Sometimes I don't have to travel very far. My inspections are in my hometown of Wendell.

This is where I learned to beware of any crawl space openings under a house that lack a door or cover. I stood on the lawn of the old stucco house and peered into the access. Leaves and debris-covered ground. I paused.

A more careful gaze revealed that the leaves were stirring. I took a breath and ventured in. The dead foliage and trash began moving at a rapid pace. I quickly backed out. My written report stated. "I did not enter the crawl space due to dangerous, suspicious activity. Recommend further evaluation."

The buyer of the house later contacted me and said. "We had the crawl space investigated. The investigator found several dens of snakes and had the infestation taken care of."

This was not the Rexburg "snake house" (see ABC June 16, 2011 report). Still, the buyers were sure appreciative of "The inspectors" observation.

In my 20 years of performing home inspections, I've only refused to do two inspections. The one in Jerome was so badly dilapidated it should have been condemned. I also declined a job in Burley.

The realtor met me at the property. She introduced me to the renter and then headed to her next appointment. I set my tool bag down on the living room floor, and a pungent odor caught my attention. I surveyed the area. Lying near my feet were several piles of dog shit. The cats' meows deadened the baby's crying. Heaped high in the corner lay putrid baby diapers under a blanket of flies. Green fuzzy mold floated on the kitchen's coffee pot's dark brown brew. On the counter lies a partially maggot-covered, half-eaten burrito. That put me over the edge.

"Mam," I excused myself. "Something has come up. I have to go." I called the realtor. "Sorry... I can't do it."

There are so many stories to tell. This whopper is the most vivid nightmare.

The seller/owner's wife invited us in to start the inspection. Her husband arrived about an hour later, returning from a week-long business trip. He went down to the basement to shower; however, the lights flickered. He promptly scurried back up the stairs.

"Get the hell out of my house," he howled. He stood in front of me, his bulging neck and exploding reddened face inches away from my five-foot-six-inch shuddering soul. Chad, my son, stood behind me, wondering if he would have to engage in some sort of protection.

The man moved to the side, his massive frame filling the doorway.

"No, wait, you fix the electrical problem. You're not getting out of here until you fix the fucking problem. You're not leaving!"

I looked him in the eye and quietly responded. "I'm not an electrician."

He growled, looking down at me. "Fix it, or you're not fucking leaving."

I softly replied, tilting my head backward, staring eyeball to eyeball. "Yes, sir, I'll do what I can."

He stomped off to his office. Chad and I prevented a fire in the electrical panel- the basement lights were still flickering. I shut off the main circuit breaker. Then Chad and I removed the electrical panel cover and connected the loose wire to the basement circuit breaker. Problem solved. Goliath went down to the basement bathroom and took his shower.

Chad and I continued with the home inspection. Later he came to us and apologized for his behavior. He revealed that his RV caught on fire on his way home from his business trip, and he lost everything.

The years have thickened my skin; I'm nearly an armadillo now. Experience has taught me empathy and compassion. Honesty and diligence still do not come with combat pay.

THE PRUNING

The day before Thanksgiving. I didn't know Larry would be a sufficient cause for pruning. The isles are buzzing with shoppers at Fred Meyers. I've navigated down all the aisles and filled the big metal pushcart one item at a time. It's like a scavenger hunt to find all the goodies on the wife's list of groceries;

2 lbs. of 10% ground beef,

a gallon of whole milk,

two cartons of 12 eggs, and not one carton of 24-*very important.*

1 bag Abound Grain-free Salmon & Sweet Potatoes Recipe dog food.

3 cans of Ro-Tel diced tomatoes. Ro-Tel is underlined-*very important.*

I pick up my cell phone and call my wife. "There are three varieties of diced tomatoes. Which one?"

I'm determined to get the shopping list right this time. I'm on the hunt. I guess it's a guy thing, hunting. I stroll the rest of the isles dodging the non-licensed drivers in the get-it-quick frame of mind.

Then the real challenge is before me. Gathering the specialty olives. Before I left home, the wife suggested my daughter Karissa get these items. Like I couldn't find the right scavenger items?

I said, "I can do it. You don't have to delegate it."

So the pressure is on.

Jar of jalapeno stuffed olives,

Bottle of cheese-stuffed olives,

Jar of green olives,

3 cans of medium black olives.

I cheat a little bit and call the wife to ensure I get it right. Bingo, the list is completed. I get through the check-out and put the hunted items in the Blazer, then go back into Fred Myers and grab a cup of coffee before heading home with my treasure.

I go to the counter and pay ninety-five cents for the Seattle Best coffee. During the transaction, I catch the clerk's name tag, Larry. I wander over to the air pot dispensers around the corner, place my cup under the medium-strength coffee spout, and push the pump handle. Spitter-spatter, just air. "Ugh." I move my cup under my second choice of coffee, bold and dark. I push down the pump handle, Spitter spatter, just air. "Ugh." My face grimaces, and the hair on my neck begins to rise. I move my cup under my third choice, light and mild. I push down on the air pot dispenser handle. Spitter, spatter, just air. "arrrgh." Finally, my fourth choice is Decaf. I place my cup under the spout, push the handle, and out comes unleaded liquid. I pause for a second. "No, I'm not doing it. I'm not drinking Decaf."

I grab my empty cup and angrily head around the corner. "Hey, Larry." But then I remember wisdom. Pruning back my emotions. 'A soft answer turns away wrath, but a harsh word stirs up anger.'(Proverbs 15:1) "The coffee pots are empty. Could you make some fresh?"

Larry turned with a smile, "Been busy, be just a minute or two."

"No worries," I said. "Take your time. Fresh coffee is always worth the wait."

I wandered to the window, climbed onto the barstool, and took a breath. Feeling the fruit of an adequately pruned branch. Joy.

THREE O'CLOCK COFFEE

Am I stupid, or are they just idiots?

It's another workday. Retirement is going great. It's like saying lemons are sweet or cotton candy tastes like Sour Patch Kids. For this seasonal moment, retirement is bewildering. Anyway, time for my ritual three o'clock coffee break-a retirement benefit.

I'm in Meridian, Idaho headed north on Meridian Avenue; on my left is the Golden Arches. They have the choicest coffee, and for a senior, it's only eighty-four cents, including tax.

I order the coffee just as I like it; hot, black, and no sugar. The service is speedy today after the manager instructs the young man that someone is at the register. And he stops flirting with the redhead at the service window.

I grab my coffee at the counter and stroll to the ice dispenser. I pour out a little of the steamy black liquid and add a few chunks of ice to cool it off. "Ah, perfect."

I slide into the hard orange plastic, chromed-leg chair at the small square table near the large picture window.

The brown and green plant life outside is waving slightly, and the raindrops are splashing against the glass. Relaxed, I take a few sips of the delicious brew and then glance down at the side of the paper cup as the steamy aroma fills my nose.

The wording on the McCafe'cup catches my attention. "Richly blended coffee & expresso drinks made with 100% Arabica beans. Details inside." *Hmm, that's interesting. It seems a waste, but I need to know the details.*

I dump out the rest of my coffee. Then look intently into the paper vessel. Nothing, nope, no information. "What the heck!"

SEVEN

RUMINATIONS

SCARS

Behind every injury is a story. Scars signify healing, but some wounds don't have scars. I count eight. The wounds, the invisible ones, I'm still finding them. This is the snapshot version.

The first remembrance I have is of when I was five. I was walking down the sidewalk to visit an elderly neighbor when curiosity got me. I saw the board with the nail sticking straight up and wondered if that nail could hold my weight. To quote Forest Gump, "stupid is as stupid does." The answer is no. I can't bend over far enough to see the bottom of my foot, but I'm sure there is a dot scar there.

The scar on my shin happened when Wayne and I built a fort in the stone crusher woods. My hatchet hit a "rubber tree," and ricko-shayed off. The blade cut to the bone of my shin and laid the flesh open. I remember this because it didn't bleed. But I could see the multitude of red dots where the hair was.

The scar on my palm and the brown bruise mark on my back came from when Bill and I played army in the cow pasture. The young bull ran from the top of the hill and bounced me off the barbed wire fence until I could duck under it to escape.

Years later, in high school, I was at a nighttime ice skating party at the flats, a large flooded meadow. When Sheryl ran over my hand with her figure skate. That left a scar, barely visible now, on the top of the right hand's middle finger knuckle.

The scar on the top of my right thigh came when I cut ridge shingles while re-roofing my house. I cut the shingles laid across my leg with my razor utility knife. I thought, this is not good, but a split second too late, the blade sliced through the shingle and my leg just as I knew.

The last self-inflicted wound I remember happened a few years ago. After mowing the lady's lawn, I pick up the lawnmower and put it on the bed of my truck. My wrist pressed against the hot muffler. The muscular fatty tissue turned to blistering and peeling.

I used to boast that I had never broken a bone or had to have stitches. Then came the gallstones, surgery, stitches, and scars.

Some wounds have no scars because they never completely heal. The divorce. The death of a daughter. The death of my father, brother, and even a beloved pet. The injuries cure a little each year, but I don't think they will ever not hurt.

These kinds of wounds cannot be seen. Most of them can be identified. They appear unexpectedly. A voice, a hug, a holiday, a picture, a movie…

This morning I lay awake pondering the wounds. I realized that I have a healer. He gives me hope, comfort, and strength to make it through this short journey we call life. The wind blows, the storms come, but I am firmly planted. Forever.

ALMOST THERE

I consider it more now than when I was a child. As a child, I didn't think, "I'm almost there." Unless I was going someplace with mom and dad. Back then, the phrase was, "Are we there yet?"

Through the dripping dew covering my eyes, I see a fork in the road, a wide paved lane on the left, and a skinny rocky path on the right. Now that I'm over the hill, I occasionally ponder my journey. Hmm, "I'm almost there."

My wife, Linda, says, "Glenn, you're not even close, so don't go there in your head."

Some of my loved ones and friends are already there. They don't have to say, "I'm almost there."

My first loved one is my brother Ted. What a trooper. He fought mightily. Everything was a struggle from the beginning, his ability to walk, talk, feed himself… What enemy could be so cruel? But he prevailed. Victory is his.

I look over the horizon, squinting my eyes; it's so far away I cannot see it clearly. The problem is I don't know when I will arrive. I know, "I'm almost there." But when I look in the mirror, I see my head tilted, my fist pressed against my chin, lips, and cheek, distorting my face. And my eyes cocked to one side.

My daughter, Lori, didn't plan on making it there so soon. Her journey began before elementary school; adversaries were abundant. Open flesh-eating wounds, devouring her little by little. They messed with her brain until… What a warrior, but now, victory. She doesn't have to say, "I'm almost there."

My dad, Willy, what a dude. Five-foot-two inches tall, his pant leg inseam measures twenty-six inches, and his shoe size- is five double D or E. There is not a mightier man. Determined, strong-willed, and didn't take shit from anyone. Once, he even brought back the neighbor's dog shit deposited on our lawn and put it on the neighbor's back porch. He is not a candidate if there is a trophy for making many friends.

He worked three jobs if that's what it took to provide. He retired at age eighty-two. He was so pissed at the one deceitful culprit he could not beat; Leukemia. Dad doesn't have to say, "I'm almost there."

My in-laws, Ray and Marion, born in Wisconsin, moved around a lot. I know they said, "We're almost there," more times than the number of trout in the river. Before I met, my wife, Ray, and Marion lived in four states, residing at twenty-one separate locations.

So they said, "We are almost there," until the choice was not theirs anymore.

In 2018 Linda and I celebrated our Twenty-fifth wedding anniversary. We left home for a three-week fun trip to drive Route 66. We departed Wendell to Joliet, Illinois, and got on Mother Road. Twenty-five hundred miles later, we arrived in Santa Monica, California. We arrived in time to watch a glorious sunset, smell the fragrance of salt air, listen to crashing waves and feel the sand between our toes. Totally awesome. We kissed. Then we strolled over to the pier and snapped a picture of the "End of 66" sign. We left the dock and headed to Las Vegas. After several hours on the blacktop the next day, headed home, we said, "We're almost there."

"Almost there" is a phrase I have said many times. In fear, like headed to divorce counseling. With joy, like going to the altar with my new bride-to-be.

Mom does her daily routine. Gets up and goes to the bathroom using her walker. Gets herself ready for the day most days. Cooks her egg whites and takes her supplements, fifteen of them or more (I never did count them, but it's a bunch), and her meds. She sits at the kitchen table for most of the day, where everything she needs to function is within arm's reach.

Mom says, "I'm ninety-one years old. I didn't plan on being here this long." She is "almost there" She is ready, but I don't want her to go. I'm not prepared for that.

Many of my loved ones, friends, and others I know can't say, "Almost there." To name a few; Grandpa Myhr, Grandpa Theberge, Grandma Theberge, Henry, Evan, Eugene, Pauline, Teresa, Joe, Robert, Gerry, Steve's father… My daughter April and Grandson Maxx almost could not say "almost there" anymore.

Some of my loved ones had no choice- a disease, old age, guns, accidents, or other robbers of this earthly life made a choice for them. Others made a choice- alcohol, drugs, guns, stupidity.

I'm "almost there," but I'm unsure when I will arrive. When I do, it's best described through the lyrics of "I Can Only Imagine" by one of my beloved artists, Mercy Me.

I will not have to say, "Almost there" anymore. But until then, I'm here, loving life.

GOING TO SLEEP

I lay on my back to go to sleep. Silicone pressed over my nose and mouth. Air was being forced down my throat into my lungs.

The mask muffled my scream, "I can't breathe." I grabbed the covering, ripped it off my face, and threw it against the wall.

I said to my wife, Linda. "I hate this freakin thing."

My first pair of eyeglasses was forty-nine years ago. They fell out of my shirt pocket while leaning out the car door. I backed up and ran over them. I didn't get another pair for twenty-nine years. Three years ago, I replaced my eyeglasses with expensive transition lenses. I spent my whole social security check for them. I took four trips back and forth to Ann's, Boutique to adjust them properly. She is awesome. I told her that I would be her problem child.

She responded. "I love challenges; I specialize in problem children."

The first week I had my hearing aids- worth a pair of diamond earrings, I lost one. I was all suited up in my home inspection coveralls, gloves, N-95 face masks, glasses, spider stick, and stocking cap. The left hearing aid must have flown out of my ear when I removed my hat. I searched for hours under leaves, dirt, and debris. Fortunately, the audiologist, Fritz, told me there was insurance for the loss. He could replace it for ninety dollars.

Sometimes the tiny rubber wax protector at the end of the hearing aid comes off and gets lodged out of sight in my ear canal. It takes a skilled physician or a loving wife and tweezers to find and remove it.

I had forgotten that dried leaves crunch and birds tweet. I discovered a unique quality in my wife's singing voice. Another "benefit" is hearing my wife while driving the car.

Five years ago, Linda couldn't sleep. She would lay awake most of the night, checking on me. I lay there snoring and gasping for air.

"Glenn, wake up, wake up. You're not breathing." She kept hounding me.

Finally, she convinced me to see Doctor Doyle at Saint Luke's. Then the sleep lab and the C-Pap store. Dr. Doyle also set up an appointment to see a sleep specialist, Dr. Armra. Everyone calls her Dr. Armra because her last name is too hard to pronounce. Dr. Armra's diagnosis was centralized sleep apnea. A special kind of sleep apnea.

"It's a brain issue." She said. Centralized in my head. She is kind; she didn't call me her problem child.

After many visits to the apnea clinicians and changing providers, a C-pap was not the device I needed. I needed a particular breathing device for a problem child, an ASV machine. Also, I am a mouth breather- I don't normally breathe through my nose when I sleep. So I need a full face cushion mask.

Almost every night, I put the damn thing on. I'm supposed to wear it for at least four hours. Every year, Dr. Amra and I discuss this when I see her for an evaluation.

She says, "You could die before your time, wear the mask." It's been a while since I've ripped the damn thing off my face; I've learned self-control. Though that's not the purpose of the pressurized full-face covering breathing machine. I am still alive. But my wife, Linda, still does not sleep well. My tossing, turning, mumbling, and cussing keep her from getting a good night's sleep. The machine pumps out a force of air that creates a whistle and a small hurricane that blows across the bed at night. I manage to sleep through most of this until it becomes so severe I want to rip it off my face and throw it against the wall. But I just "gently" remove it, roll over, and go back to sleep. Unless Linda wakes me up because I'm not breathing. Dr. Amra also prescribed sleeping pills; I take them every night.

I think back to the time I went for a colonoscopy. The anesthesiologist gave me some Propofol. That was the best sleep I ever had. But that has to be given under professional supervision.

Sleeping, hearing, seeing, breathing; life is like a hurdle race for me. Computers, smartphones, motorcycle licensee test, navigation… what next?

A NEW LIFE

The tale that keeps nagging me to put on paper. In high school, in my sophomore and junior year, Bob and I went to midnight Mass at St. Joseph's Catholic Church. We thought being up that late and going to church was cool. This also allowed Bob to skip Christmas morning Mass. However, I was uneasy, walking into that vast ornate sanctuary; the stained glass windows, the candles, the pews, men in robes, and the scent of Frankincense and Myrrh. Also, do the cross sign at the entrance with the holy water. I mimicked Bob, who went before me. Dipping my right-hand fingers in the font, touching my forehead, then the top of my stomach, then from right to left while mumbling the blessing. Then there was the kneeling and standing and making the crucifix sign at the proper times and….

Moreover, the sermon was in Latin. Who knows Latin? But I did know Christmas was about the birth of Jesus.

At 20, I married Cathy, who wanted to be married in the Catholic Church, but I couldn't because I was not confirmed or had my first confession. I agreed to confirmation classes with Father Johnson. I checked all the right boxes and made my first confession in that small wooden dark closet, where a small black curtain separated him and me. I confessed dreadful things; lying, stealing, and God's name in vain. He kept prompting and probing me, sexual sins, on and on. All that I could remember. It would make a pretty raunchy book. Cathy and I were married by a Catholic Priest at a Chelsea Naval Base chapel. On the day of marriage, we set out from Massachusetts to California, my mother's 41st. Birthday.

The thoughts of my mind and heart became void of God for many years. And I was not very proud of some things in my life. My door-to-door photo plan sales practice had some deception and dishonesty. My moral life was tainted with visits to "massage parlors," which could be called brothels. Pornography was enjoyable. Fortunately, drugs were not part of my lifestyle. Financial problems grew.

Then strange things began happening in my life; one family I pitched the photo plan to talked to me about being Saved. Other random people approached me with questions about salvation and Jesus. This went on for several weeks. The conversations were very annoying.

At the end of December 1973, my first son, Aaron, was born. In January 74, he was hospitalized with pneumonia. Cathy and I were very nervous and concerned. In addition to Aaron's hospitalization, Cathy injured her back and was bedridden. One evening I knelt in our darkened bedroom and prayed, "Dear God, help me, please help me. If you are there, if you can hear me, please help. I don't know what to do. I don't know".

A few days later, the assistant Pastor from the El Cajon Fletcher Hills Bible Church came to visit and pray for us. That night, Pastor Bob Ignot prayed for our family and shared a small booklet called the "four spiritual laws." Bob invited us to a small home Bible study at Steve's and Teresa's. My only Bible was a large three-pound illustrated family Bible on our coffee table. It was very awkward; I was totally in the dark about the Bible and only a little familiar with Catholic beliefs. We studied Mark's Gospel verse by verse and chapter by chapter. I was very defensive of my limited Catholic beliefs. We talked about what the Bible said about Jesus. I began to search for God. Weeks later, I discovered that our cousins, Steve and Teresa, had been praying for us for quite some time.

Being born again has changed my life. I've repented from my old ways. Like God says, I am a new creature, the old has passed away, and the new has begun. He has given me a new focus. I've moved from unaware to aware. Convicted and repentant, seeking and loving God. The journey of new life. I've been on this journey for more than 45 years now.

Life is not without troubles or problems. I don't know what weird thing happens in the head when a person is about forty. Cathy decided to start a different new life. She ran off. Well, actually, the woman didn't run away. She asked me to take her to the bus stop to visit her ailing dad in North Carolina. I didn't know it was going to be a no-return ticket. I became Mr. Mom for a while, caring for our children, cleaning the house, doing laundry... I got domesticated.

So after 23 years, our relationship ended in divorce. Loneliness set in, and I began to pray that God would help me find a Godly wife. Lo and behold. My prayer came true. In 1993 I met a beautiful young lady, Linda.

Actually, I met Linda several years ago when our church played volleyball. At that time, I was happily married to Cathy. But I remember looking forward to seeing Linda in the gym on volleyball nights. Adorable, petite, long silky hair, and tight sexy Scuzi jeans. I loved watching her. Cathy hired her to do light housekeeping. Until after Linda and I got married, I didn't know that Linda admired me as a husband and father, hoping she would marry someone like me someday. After my divorce, Linda and I dated for 6 months before we got married. She loves the Lord. She is the joy of my life. In September 2019, we celebrated our 25th. Anniversary. I also gained two more beautiful children.

EIGHT

LOOKING UP

BOOK ENDS

Somewhere in my life's journey, the apathy bush became my cover. I'm getting better. I've been working on that issue for more than 25 years. My wife, Linda, is instrumental in pruning away the branches to let in the light. I'm not a psychiatrist, so I don't understand why I'm like this or how I got here.

Jesus is the heartbeat of my life and has been since January 1974. I struggle with writing because the events I tell my kids about are things I did before my relationship with God. My walk with the Lord is by far not perfect. I want to be authentic. I think most of my Christian friends would frown at the language. I don't consider myself a typical Christian if there is such a label. I see God's hand on me throughout my life. Some may think the lesser of me because of my crudeness.

I quit church (lowercase c) several years ago. Because people spend more time in disagreement and seeking places of position and power rather than being and doing what Jesus, God, wants to be done. It's not about church.

It's about being a Christian, loving and serving God and others. I strive to be the person of character God wants me to be. I'm not against the Church. I just don't want to be a part of the institution.

I hope that after all my life experiences and stories are read, the hand of God will be seen in my life's journey. I'm 73 years old. I think about my life ending more often than in my younger years. My love for God and my relationship with Him is the legacy I want to leave behind. My journey, for now, continues until they throw dirt on my coffin. I am joyful that I answered when He knocked on the door of my heart.

Silence is a scary place. It's not for the timid. The dense cloud of noise and activity is my enemy. But when I find shelter near the quiet water, I hear His voice the loudest.

Knock, Knock.